Treatment of Depression in Children & Adolescents

Connie Callahan, Ph.D., LPCC, LMFT

PESI Publishing & Media
www.pesi.com/publishing

Copyright © 2009 by Connie Callahan, Ph.D., LPCC, LMFT
Published by
PESI, Inc.
3839 White Ave
Eau Claire, WI 54703

Printed in the United States of America

ISBN: 978-0-9820398-3-0

PESI Publishing & Media
ww.pesi.com/publishing

About the Author

Connie Callahan, Ph.D., LPCC, LMFT, is the Chair of the Counseling and Educational Psychology Department at Eastern Kentucky University. She has practiced as a Licensed Professional Clinical Counselor and a Licensed Marriage and Family Therapist since 1986 in a variety of settings. Dr. Callahan has been using researched based interventions with clients, supervisees, and colleagues in various treatment settings and graduate programs for over two decades, and is known nationally as an expert trainer, clinical supervisor, clinician and acclaimed PESI presenter.

Dr. Callahan has worked with dozens of clinicians and organizations to integrate researched based interventions in clinical practices and program models. She has over 30 years in mental health treatment settings across all levels of care. Dr. Callahan provides licensure supervision and collegial consultation to mental health, school and dual diagnosis clinicians. She also works with systems of care and individual clinicians to implement and sustain evidenced based practices with a variety of mental disorders. She publishes regularly in journals and books.

Table of Contents

Preface   7

Chapter 1: Major Depressive Disorder   9

Chapter 2: Short Term Goals: The Dynamic Role of Feelings,
    Thoughts, and Behaviors that Contribute to Depression   25

Chapter 3: Counseling Interventions: Reducing the Symptoms of Depression   57

Conclusion   139

References   141

Preface

This book examines incidence rates, diagnostic and statistical categories, best practice guidelines and practical treatment interventions for depressive disorders relating to children and adolescents. Studies in adults and one study in youth have suggested that each successive generation since 1940 is at greater risk for developing depressive disorders, and that these disorders are being recognized at a younger age (Kovacs and Gatsonis, 1994; Ryan et al., 1992). In 2002–2003, President Bush issued an Executive Order to create the President's New Freedom Commission on Mental Health. The commission (2003) produced a final report entitled: *Achieving the Promise: Transforming Mental Health Care in America*, which built on the existing research in the field, the Surgeon General's report on Mental Health and the Institute of Medicine's report on *Crossing the Quality Chasm: Health Care for the 21st Century*. Some of the key findings the Commission drew from these reports included these facts:

- 20% of adults and children have a diagnosable mental health problem.
- Of these 20%, half have a serious emotional disorder that incapacitates functioning in at least two domains of their life (e.g., school, work, family, etc.).
- 10–13% of preschoolers (ages 1–6 years old) have emotional or behavioral disorders.
- About 20 million children and adults in the U.S. suffer from serious disabling mental illness.
- Suicide: There are approximately 30,000 suicides a year (more than homicides).
- Among adolescents 15–19 years old, suicide is the 3rd leading cause of death; 17–19% think about killing themselves; 5–8% make an attempt; only 1/3 get treatment.
- States spend over $1 billion on medical costs associated with suicides and suicide attempts by youth under age 20 (NGA, 2005).

Only half of individuals with serious mental disorders get treatment, services or supports. As a result: (1) there is a tremendous individual, family and societal burden of untreated mental health disorders and (2) the cost of mental health care has shifted to systems that are more costly and are not designed to provide mental health services. For example:

- Of children with serious emotional/behavioral disorders: approximately 50% dropout of high school, compared to 30% of students with other disabilities (U.S. Department of Education, 2001).

- Of youth entering Juvenile Justice: 66–75% have serious emotional problems (Teplin, 2002).

- Of the approximately 500,000 children in foster care, of whom about 44% are under five years of age, it is estimated that 40–80% have an emotional behavioral and/or substance abuse problem (AFGARS/US DHHS, 2003).

- More than one-third of children served by a major federal community mental health services grant program have a co-occurring disorder with the pattern being a diagnosis of a mental disorder around age 11 and a substance abuse disorder being diagnosed six to seven years later around ages 17–18 (Kessler et al., 1996; Center for Mental Health Services/ORC Macro, 2004).

No one group of mental health workers can deal with this crisis alone. Schools by themselves and mental health agencies alone cannot, and should not be expected to, address the nation's most serious health and social problems. Families, health care workers, the media, religious organizations, and community organizations that serve people must be systematically involved.

Too often in counseling and psychology, a mental health practitioner adheres to a theoretical philosophy in the treatment of young persons rather than paying attention to presented symptoms and researched best practice guidelines. When there are guidelines available, the practitioner often has no sure guidance in turning theory into therapy for children and adolescents. While this is not the definitive work in that process, practical strategies and interventions are offered with a research base.

Best practice guidelines are normally offered in professional journals under the guise of "practice parameters." These are strategies for patient management, developed to assist clinicians in psychiatric decision-making. These parameters, based on evaluation of the scientific literature and relevant clinical consensus, describe generally accepted approaches to assess and treat specific disorders, or to perform specific medical procedures. The validity of scientific findings was judged by design, sample selection and size, inclusion of comparison groups, the ability to generalize, and agreement with other studies.

Best practice parameters are not intended to define the standard of care and although they should not be deemed inclusive of all proper methods of care, they are devised to help mental health practitioners in obtaining the efficacious treatment results. The ultimate judgment regarding the care of a particular patient must be made by the clinician in light of all the circumstances presented by the patient and his or her family, the diagnostic and treatment options available and available resources.

CHAPTER 1
Major Depressive Disorder

According to the National Action Agenda for Children's Mental Health (Canton, 2001), one in ten adolescents—or as many as 8 million young people—suffer from a mental disorder. In any given year, only one in five receives any mental health care, according to a new report released by the US Surgeon's General office. David Satcher, M.D., Ph.D., Assistant Secretary for Health and Surgeon General provided insight into this problem.

By the year 2020, childhood neuropsychiatric problems—which include depression, attention deficit disorder, and anxiety disorders, such as social phobia and obsessive-compulsive disorder—will increase by more than 50%. Depressive disorders are leading causes of morbidity and mortality in young people. The prevalence of major depressive disorders is estimated to be approximately 2% in children and 4 to 8% in adolescents. Although occurring at approximately the same rate in girls and boys during childhood, a 2-to-1 ratio becomes evident during adolescence.

Some researchers view depression in youth as a significant problem that affects approximately 30% of the adolescent population (Lewinsohn, Hops, Roberts, Seeley, & Andrew, 1993). In fact, one in five youngsters report a minimum of one episode of major depression by the age of 18 (Lewinsohn et al., 1993). The prevalence of a major depressive disorder is estimated to be approximately 2% in children and 4% to 8% in adolescents with a male/female ratio of 1:1 during childhood and 1:2 during adolescence (Fleming and Offord, 1990; Kashani et al., 1987a,b; Lewinsohn et al., 1994a). The cumulative incidence by age 18 is approximately 20% in community samples (Lewinsohn et al., 1993a).

According to the National Action Agenda for Children's Mental Health, the nation lacks a unified infrastructure to help children with mental disorders, and many are falling through the cracks. Too often, children who are not identified as having mental health problems end up in jail. Each year, more than 2,000 young people commit suicide, the third leading cause of death among 15 to 24-year-olds (following motor vehicle crashes and homicide). At the very least, mental disorders like depression interfere with education and social interactions and keep children from realizing their full potential as adults.

The Surgeon General has recommended The National Action Agenda to begin to deal with this problem. The National Action Agenda identifies eight goals and strategies to improve services for children and adolescents with mental health problems and their families. One of the report's key recommendations is reducing the stigma associated with mental illness

Parents are often fearful about bringing the social and emotional difficulties of children to the attention of medical professionals. They are afraid they may be blamed. Children are sometimes directly stigmatized by the cruelty of classmates. The report calls for a public education campaign to promote awareness of children's mental health issues accomplished through partnerships with media, youth, communities, health professionals, and advocacy groups. One way to begin this process is to make sure that practitioners understand and use scientifically proven prevention and treatment strategies in dealing with youth.

Prevention and Treatment

Developing, Disseminating, and Implementing Scientifically Proven Prevention and Treatment Services in the Field of Children's Mental Health.

Scientific knowledge of the brain has grown at an unprecedented rate. In the field of child mental health, science has been far ahead of clinical care. There is research on proven treatments, practices, and services developed in the laboratory to help with the war against mental illness. We need to bridge the gap between research and practice. Surgeon General Satcher advocates a forum for promoting communication among researchers, providers, youth, and families, with a special workgroup convened to monitor progress of psychopharmacology for children.

The Counselor's Role

The Surgeon General's Report clearly emphasizes the role of school counselors, mental health counselors, social workers, psychologists and other mental health practitioners in the National Action Agenda. This report notes that school counselors and teachers are in a good position to recognize depression in children with a little training in the matter and that counselors may be part of a treatment team to manage the disorder, along with other mental health professionals who can prescribe medications and other agencies who may help alleviate stressors on children and families. However, counselors need to be aware of and use proven strategies and guidelines to assist children in a school setting. Those guidelines are provided in a variety of journals.

The Disorder

For purposes of this discussion, the focus is on the symptoms, not the diagnosis of depressive episodes. **The DSM-IV-TR Criteria for Major Depressive Episode** by the American Psychiatric Association (2000, page 356) include five or more symptoms from the following list. The symptoms must have been present for the same two week period and they must represent a change in the previous functioning of the individual. Also the child or adolescent must either demonstrate a depressed mood or loss of interest or pleasure.

The symptoms include:

1. Depressed mood most of the day, nearly every day, as indicated by either subjective report (e.g., feels sad or empty) or observation made by others (e.g., appears tearful) but in children and adolescents, this can be an irritable mood.

2. Markedly diminished interest or pleasure in all, or almost all, activities most of the day, nearly every day (as indicated by either subjective account or observation made by others).

3. Significant weight loss when not dieting or weight gain (e.g., a change of more than 5% of body weight in a month), or decrease or increase in appetite nearly every day and in children failure to make expected weight gain would be a symptom.

4. Insomnia or hypersomnia nearly every day

5. Psychomotor agitation or retardation nearly every day (observable by others, not merely subjective feelings of restlessness or being slowed down).

6. Fatigue or loss of energy nearly every day.

7. Feelings of worthlessness or excessive or inappropriate guilt (which may be delusional) nearly every day (not merely self-approach or guilt about being sick).

8. Diminished ability to think or concentrate, or indecisiveness, nearly every day (either by subjective account or as observed by others).

9. Recurrent thoughts of death (not just fear of dying), recurrent suicidal ideation without a specific plan, or a suicide attempt or a specific plan for committing suicide.

10. The depressive symptoms cannot be better accounted for by other disorders like Schizoaffective Disorder, Schizophrenia, Schizophreniform Disorder, Delusional Disorder, or Psychotic Disorder Not Otherwise Specified and there has never been a manic, mixed or hypomanic episode.

Dysphoria Not Always Evident

Children and adolescents with depression may present for treatment because of problems that are not initially evident as depression. For example, children may present with nonspecific physical complaints (stomachache, headache) or because of a negative irritable mood leading to oppositional behaviors and refusal to do school work or attend school. In adolescents, the presenting problem may be suicidal thoughts or behaviors or antisocial behavior, including substance abuse.

Child and Adolescent Depression

The DSM-IV delineates aspects of adolescent depressive symptoms as opposed to common symptoms experienced by adults. Symptom delineation has been made between prepubescent children and adolescents. For example, children commonly display irritable mood rather than depressed mood, somatic complaints, and social withdrawal. Depressed adolescents typically display psychomotor retardation and hypersomnia.

A clinician would need to understand that the manifestation of childhood depression will be very different in various developmental levels and in diverse ethnic groups but there will be similar symptoms to adult depressive disorder (Birmaher, et al., 1996a; Kovacs, 1996; Mitchell et al., 1988; Ryan et al., 1987). Children usually show more symptoms of anxiety (including phobias and separation anxiety), somatic complaints, and auditory hallucinations (Chambers et al., 1982; Mitchell et al., 1988; Ryan et al., 1987). Also, children may express irritability and frustration with temper tantrums and behavioral problems instead of verbalizing feelings.

In contrast, adolescents tend to display more sleep and appetite disturbances, delusions, suicidal ideation and attempts. They also function in a more impaired fashion than younger children and exhibit behavioral problems.

Capuzzi and Ross (1999) in a book, *Youth at Risk: A Prevention Resource for Counselors, Teachers, and Parents,* discussed the DSM-IV the fact that depressed children also manifest symptoms of other disorders along with depression. They stated that the DSM-IV noted that prepubertal children typically display major depressive episodes in conjunction with disruptive behavior disorders, attention-deficit disorders, and anxiety disorders. Adolescent depression is more commonly associated with disruptive behavior disorders, attention-deficit disorders, anxiety disorders, substance-related disorders, and eating disorders.

Dr. Goldman (1999), a Diplomat of the American Board of Psychiatry and Neurology, has identified adult depressive symptoms, child and adolescent symptoms of Depressive Disorder. In his article, he includes a chart that identifies behaviors that might be manifested in different age groups.

Adult Symptom	Child Example	Adolescent Example
Depressed/sad mood	Irritable, argumentative, aggressive, whining/crying	Argumentative, aggressive, emotionally sensitive
Diminished interest/pleasure, inability to feel pleasure	Not as motivated or playful, not as curious and explorative, school work drops off, boredom	Isolative, quits activities, shows no initiative, grades drop, boredom
Unintentional weight changes	Fails to gain weight normally	Weight changes
Sleep changes	Difficulty falling asleep or staying asleep	Difficulty falling asleep or staying asleep, stays up all night
Being slowed down or sped up	Difficulty concentrating or sitting still, impulsivity, less active or interactive, hyperactive, disorganized	Difficulty concentrating or sitting still, impulsivity, less active or interactive, disorganized
Fatigue	Needs rests, naps, complains when is pushed to do things, plays "sick"	Refuses to participate, lays around a lot, sleeps during day, acts "sick" a lot
Worthlessness and guilt	Makes negative self-comments such as "You hate me" and "I'm stupid"	Makes negative self comments such as "I'm fat" "I'm ugly" "Everybody hates me"
Poor concentration, can't make decisions	Poor attention and concentration, easily distractible, disorganized	Poor attention and concentration, easily distractible
Thoughts of death or suicide	Talks about death, states "I wish I was never born" or "I wish I was dead"	Obsesses on death and morbid topics, voices wishes to be dead or thinks about/attempts suicide
Psychosis: hearing things, seeing things, or paranoia	Extreme fears for safety, seeing scary images, hearing monsters	Suspiciousness, paranoia, seeing fearful images or hearing their name called

Treatment

Treatment of depression should be individualized and based on need, resources and assessment of stressors involved in a particular case. Psychotherapy is an essential component of an individualized treatment plan and cognitive-behavioral therapy and interpersonal therapy have been deemed efficacious in the treatment of depression, often in conjunction with medication. Counselors can offer supportive treatment. In many cases, however, neither medication nor psychotherapy alone will be sufficient to handle the symptoms of major depression in children and adolescents.

Clinical Course

There are several terms used to describe the various stages of a depressive disorder. Following a medical model, the stages include the terms response, remission, partial remission, recovery, relapse, and recurrence. Response is used when a client is receiving treatment and it is used to signify the improvement of symptoms. Remission is a period of time when a client goes two weeks and less than two months with no more than one clinically significant symptom. Partial remission is when a client has more than one clinically significant depressive symptom but is not evidencing a full blown depressive syndrome. Recovery is when a patient has no symptoms for more than two months. Relapse can occur if a patient has been in remission and then has an episode of depression. Recurrence is the emergence of symptoms of major depressive disorder during the period of recovery.

A clinician will need to take a full psychosocial history of both a youth and his or her family to determine the typical clinical course of this disorder for the patient. Of specific interest would be any attempts made at suicide. The adolescent rate of suicide has quadrupled since 1950 (2.5 to 11.2 per 100,000), and currently represents 12% of the total mortality in this age group (Lewinsohn et al., 1993b). In this assessment, the clinician will need to specifically ask questions concerning:

- past suicide attempts
- family history of mood disorders
- family history of suicidal behavior
- exposure to family violence
- exposure to abuse
- impulsivity
- availability of lethal agents (e.g., firearms)
- substance use

(Brent et al., 1993; Brent, 1995; Fergusson et al., 1996)

The assessment also should include information gathered about specific socio-environmental circumstances, including family history of suicidal behavior, poor parent-child communication, school problems, and negative life events (Gould et al., 1996).

Assessment

The comprehensive psychiatric diagnostic evaluation is the single most useful tool currently available to diagnose depressive disorders. For a detailed description and recommendations on psychiatric evaluation of children and adolescents, see Practice Parameters for the Psychiatric Assessment of Children and Adolescents (American Academy of Child and Adolescent Psychiatry,

1997). Assessment should be ongoing, and the interventions should be tailored to meet the needs of the child or adolescent in all phases of the depressive disorder.

During assessment, it is imperative for the clinician to be alert to ethnic and cultural factors that may influence the presentation, description, or interpretation of symptoms and the approach to treatment. A clinician should study the culture of a client to avoid misreading cultural teachings as symptoms of depression. For example, children from many cultures are encouraged to be silent and to avoid direct eye contact when in the presence of authority figures. These behaviors easily could be misinterpreted as indicators of depression, anxiety, or another psychiatric disorder.

A mood lifetime chart, using school years as anchors, and a mood diary are very helpful in the assessment of mood disorders. Mood is rated from very happy to very sad, and/or very irritable to non-irritable, and stressors are noted. The chart can help the child visualize the course of her or his illness and identify events that may have triggered the depression. How such a chart is created and used would depend on the age of the child and would best be devised using various counseling interventions discussed in later chapters. For example, a six-year-old child may need to be taught expressions of various moods before he or she can participate in the development of a mood chart. Any time a child or adolescent is involved in the therapy process in any manner besides talking and answering questions leads to more effective clinical outcomes.

Several self-administered and clinician-administered rating scales, such as the Beck Depression Inventory (BDI) (Marton et al., 1991), the Child Depression Inventory (CDI) (Kovacs, 1992), and The Center for Epidemiologic Studies Depression Scale (CES-D) (Roberts et al., 1991), can be used to screen for symptoms, assess the severity of depressive symptoms, and monitor clinical improvement. Each would need to be matched to the age and ability of the child or adolescent.

After the Assessment

As early as possible, the counselor should engage both the youth and the family in treatment. Eardslee et al, (1997) and Fristad, et al (1996) stressed the importance of educating the family about depression. Beasrslee et al (1997) indicated that the symptoms of depression such as lack of interest, fatigue, irritability, and isolation create problems for the entire family and that such issues can be addressed to foster a better therapeutic alliance between the counselor and client. Topics may include the signs and symptoms of depression, the role of psychiatric medication, common misconceptions about medications, relapse and recurrence, impact on school attendance and academic functioning, the role of the parents and teachers in recovery, and impact on peer and family relationships. Treatment chapters in this book will provide specific educational materials that may be used in such educational activities.

Based on the clinical experience and the few child and adolescent randomized treatment studies available, psychotherapy appears to be a useful initial acute treatment for mild to moderate depression (Geller, 1994). Cognitive-behavioral therapy (CBT) has been studied extensively.

CBT and interpersonal therapy are two of the most frequently studied psychotherapy treatments. Interpersonal theory focuses on the relationship between the therapist and the client. CBT efficacy for major depressive disorder is based on the premise that depressed patients have a distorted view of themselves, the world, and the future. The distorted thinking of depressed children and adolescents contribute to their depression and can be identified and counteracted with CBT. Four studies have shown group CBT to be better than no intervention for children and adolescents in the reduction of depressive symptomatology and improvement of self-esteem (Kahn et al., 1990; Lewinsohn et al., 1990; Reynolds and Coates, 1986; Reinecke et al., 1998). In most clinical samples, CBT has been found to be superior to other treatments (Brent et al., 1997; Kroll et al., 1996; Vostanis et al., 1996), and CBT is therefore recommended as a best practice in the treatment of depression in children and adolescents. It should be noted that in many cases psychotherapy alone is not sufficient to treat a major depressive disorder. However, how to use medications and what medications to use with children and adolescents have been difficult to determine.

Drug Therapy

Controlled studies of the efficacy of depression in youth are difficult to pursue for pragmatic reasons. Often such studies offer small sample sizes making the results difficult to generalize. In controlled studies, some of the children would be given a placebo and others would be given real medicine and this would raise ethical concerns. Consequently, there are very few randomized controlled treatment trials and few open uncontrolled studies with adults (Thase and Rush, 1995) and youth. There are very few studies on the use of medications for youth with a major depressive disorder and these studies are open or have methodological problems (Mandoki et al., 1997; Ryan et al., 1988; Wilens et al., 1997).

For patients requiring pharmacotherapy, selective serotonin (5-hydroxytryptamine; 5-HT) reuptake inhibitors (SSRIs) are the antidepressants of choice given their safety, side effects profile, ease of use, and suitability for long-term maintenance. Fluoxetine (Prozac), Sertraline (Zoloft), Paroxetine (Paxil), Fluvoxamine (Luvox), and Citalopram (Celexa) are SSRIs. Given the psychosocial context in which depression unfolds, pharmacotherapy is never sufficient as the sole treatment. There is evidence that the environmental and social problems associated with major depressive disorder remain when the patient's mood has been stabilized with medication-only treatment. Combined treatment increases the likelihood not only of mitigating depressive symptomalogy, but also of increasing self-esteem, coping skills, and adaptive strategies and improving family and peer relationships.

The following information should be stressed to parents and young patients about to embark on medication therapies. The use of medications may reduce depressive symptoms enough to improve quiz and test scores, to improve visual memory and learning, to increase the accuracy and amount of student work, to decrease frustration, and to increase attention span in academic and job performance. However, medications will not improve comprehension, replace core skills missed in the past, change attitudes of about feeling like a failure or correct learning disabilities, supply the will to conform or comply, motivate a student to achieve goals, teach anyone where to place attention, or teach a student how to relax. These would be skills taught by parents, teachers, and counselors.

If Drug Therapy Is the Next Step

If a decision has been made to use pharmacological treatment, an appropriated antidepressant should be chosen using four criteria:

- the patient's subtype of depression (e.g., atypical, seasonal, or bipolar depression)
- chronicity of symptoms
- past treatment history
- the medication's likelihood of causing adverse effects, safety in overdosing and cost

A good source for those details is *Depression in Primary Care: Vol. 1, Treatment of Major Depression* from 1998. This publication is part of a series, *Clinical Practice Guidelines* from the U.S. Department of Health and Human Services, the Agency for Health Care Policy and Research.

What Parents Should Know

Before using antidepressants, parents and patients should be informed about adverse effects, dosage and the lag time before onset of therapeutic effects. A mental health professional should discuss this with parents or guardians.

Warning

According to Findling, Reed, and Blumer (1999), because of lack of efficacy and the potential for life-threatening adverse effects, neither tricyclic antidepressants (TCAs) nor monoamine oxidase inhibitors (MAOIs) should be recommended for the first line of treatment of depression in children and adolescents. Because of disappointing results and the significant potential for adverse effects with tricyclic antidepressants (TCAs) and monoamine oxidase inhibitors (MAOIs), these drug classes should be used for difficult cases where first line treatment recommendations have failed in children and adolescents. TCAs can be associated with adverse effects, some of which are potentially life-threatening. Side effects of TCAs include common anticholinergic effects of these drugs and the serious adverse effects of the TCAs include seizures and mania. Hypertension, tachycardia and confusion may also be seen.

SSRIs

Several newer medications, including the selective serotonin (5-hydroxytryptamine; 5-HT) reuptake inhibitors (SSRIs), have become the first line of medication treatment recommended for the treatment of children and adolescents.

Prozac

Fluoxetine is the most extensively studied SSRI in young people with depression. Studies have shown that treatment with Fluoxetine often leads to reductions in depressed mood. A study by Emslie, Rush, and Weinberg (1997) indicated that Fluoxetine controlled symptoms of depression in young people better than a placebo did. Most studies with positive treatment findings have involved the use of SSRIs. When the SSRIs did not work, other drugs were studied some. Two small open studies found Fluoxetine (Boulos et al., 1992) and the MAOI phenelzine (Ryan et al., 1988) to be efficacious in the treatment of adolescents who did not respond to SSRIs. Geller and colleagues (1990), in a group of adolescents with chronic and severe major depressive disorder, found that 8% responded to Nortriptyline and 21% to a placebo. In contrast, Birmaher et al. (1998) found a 70% response to Amitriptyline and a placebo in a group of adolescents with recurrent, chronic, resistant major depressive disorder. Salle et al. (1997) found that intravenous Clomipramine was superior to a placebo for adolescents with treatment-resistant depression. This short discussion about medications indicates that this is a new and much needed field of study with children and adolescents.

Venlafaxine (Effexor) and Nefazodone (Serzone) Well Tolerated

According to Findling, Reed, and Blumer (1999), Venlafaxine has been shown to be a well tolerated and effective treatment for adults with depression. Reductions in depressive symptoms were found in treatment groups and the adverse effects of Venlafaxine were generally mild. One individual who received Venlafaxine developed mania. Results from preliminary studies suggest that Nefazodone is a well tolerated and clinically effective treatment for pre-adult depression.

Tricyclics (TCAs)

Since the 1950s tricyclic medications have been the mainstay of the treatment of depression. Normally, they are not given to children and adolescents. To be sure that clinicians are familiar with them, the drug names for this type of antidepressant is listed below. However, sometimes a patient will not respond to the first line of recommended drugs, and other medications are prescribed by physicians.

Cyclic Antidepressants

Generic Name

Amitriptyline	Tofranil
Elavil	Maprotiline
Amoxapine	Ludiomil
Asendin	Pamelor
Nortriptyline	Protriptyline
Clomipramine	Vivactil
Anafranil	Trazodone
Desipramine	Desyrel
Norpramin	Trimipramine
Doxepin	Surmontil
Sinequan	Imipramine

Side Effects

The tricyclics react with a number of receptors that cause three main side effects:

1. Anticholinergic: dry mouth, dry skin, blurred vision, constipation, cessation of intestine movement, urinary retention.

2. Adrenergic: sweating, sexual dysfunction, sudysthymic disorderen drops in blood pressure upon rising, lightheadedness.

3. Antihistaminic: sedation, weight gain.

Selective Serotonin Re-uptake Inhibitors

The SSRIs are a newer class of antidepressants, and as mentioned before are the class of medications that have been most studied in youth. They have fewer side effects than tricyclics. Fluoxetine (Prozac) is typical of antidepressant agents chemically unrelated to the tricyclic, tetracyclic, or other available antidepressants. It selectively inhibits presynaptic serotonin reuptake with minimal or no effect in the reuptake of norepinephrine or dopamine.

SSRIs include:

- Fluoxetine (Prozac)

- Sertraline (Zoloft)

- Paroxetine (Paxil)

- Fluvoxamine (Luvox)

- Citalopram (Celexa)

SSRI Side Effects

The SSRI side effects are related to increased serotonin activity and include:

- Nausea

- Gastrointestinal upset

- Sweating

- Anxiety

- Insomnia

- Headache

- Restlessness

- Sexual Dysfunction

Increased physician contact and monitoring is required when using SSRIs with youths who have seizure disorder, hepatic or renal disease, or diabetes; a gradual withdrawal of at least one week is preferred when discontinuing use of SSRIs; possible serious adverse effects that require physician attention include rash or hives, seizures, and heatstroke; other possible adverse effects include nausea, diarrhea, headache, anxiety, insomnia, restlessness, dry mouth, sleepiness, tremor, excessive sweating, apathy, decreased sexual interest, weight loss, weight gain, and hypomania; caution with preexisting seizure disorders, recent myocardial infarction, unstable heart disease, and hepatic or renal impairment; decreased sexual interest is observed more commonly by report than with other SSRIs.

Monoamine Oxidase Inhibitors (MAOs)

MAO inhibitors are used mainly when other antidepressants have failed because they carry the risk of a hypertensive reaction (sudysthymic disorderen rise in blood pressure). Phenelzine (Nardil), Tranylcypromine (Parnate), Isocarboxazid (Marplan), Selegiline (Depreny) and Meclobemide are MAO inhibitors.

Atypical Antidepressants

Bupropion is a new antidepressant that is weakly serotonergic and dopamininergic and produces only two side effects (anxiety and insomnia). Venlafaxine (Effexxor) has been used for students who did not respond to other antidepressants. Its side effects include: nausea, sedation, dry mouth, dizziness and blurred vision

Mental health practitioners who work with youth on antidepressant medications would do well to devise checklists of problematic symptoms and evaluate clients from time to time to see how the medications might be affecting them. Based on the recommendations of The Pharmaceutical Press (2000) and Emslie and Mayes (1999), such checklists could follow this model:

Prozac Checklist of Possible Problems

_____   Nausea

_____   Vomiting

_____   Dyspepsia

__   Abdominal pain

_____   Diarrhea

_____   Constipation

_____   Anorexia

_____   Hypersensitivity reactions

_____   Changes in blood sugar

Possible Problems for Children on Paxil

_____   Nausea

_____   Vomiting

_____   Dyspepsia

_____   Abdominal pain

_____   Diarrhea

_____   Constipation

_____   Anorexia

_____   Hypersensitivity reactions

_____   Postural hypotension

_____   Abnormal liver function tests

Possible Problems for Children on Zoloft

_____   Nausea

_____   Vomiting

_____   Dyspepsia

_____   Abdominal pain

_____   Diarrhea

_____   Constipation

_____ Anorexia

_____ Hypersensitivity reactions

_____ Tachycardia

_____ Confusion

_____ Amnesia

_____ Hallucinations

_____ Aggressive behavior

_____ Psychosis

_____ Abnormal liver function tests

_____ Menstrual irregularities

_____ Paraesthesia

Possible Problems for Children on Effexor

_____ Nausea

_____ Headache

_____ Insomnia

_____ Somnolence

_____ Dry mouth

_____ Dizziness

_____ Constipation

_____ Asthenia

_____ Sweating

_____ Nervousness

_____ Convulsions

Antidepressants must be considered for those patients with psychosis, bipolar depression, severe depressions, and those who do not respond to an adequate trial of psychotherapy. There are phases of depression to consider in youth and other patients: the onset of symptoms and the need to continue therapy to alleviate or manage symptoms. All patients need continuation therapy and some patients may require maintenance treatment. Further research is needed on the etiology of depression; the efficacy of different types of psychotherapy; the differential effects of psychotherapy, pharmacotherapy, and integrated therapies; the continuation and maintenance treatment phases; treatment for dysthymia, treatment-resistant depression, and other subtypes of major depressive disorder; and preventive strategies for high-risk children and adolescents (The American Academy of Child and Adolescent Psychiatry, 1998).

General Conclusion

Given the prevalence of depressive disorders, prevention is of critical importance, but very few studies have been published in this area. Studies of school-aged children and adolescents with symptoms of depression have shown that cognitive behavior therapy, together with relaxation training and problem-solving therapy, may prevent recurrences of depression for up to 9 to 24 months post-treatment (Clarke et al., 1995; Jaycox et al., 1994; Lerner and Clum, 1990). Brief family-based educational interventions also have been shown to be beneficial in decreasing the effects of parental mood disorders on children at high risk for depression, although their impact on ultimate development of mood disorder is yet to be documented (Beardslee et al., 1997). Counseling activities aimed at both treatment and prevention of mood disorders in children and youths are important and should be based on best practice guidelines.

Overall, there will be some long-term goals that counselors will set for children and adolescents who are depressed. They will include the counselor and client working together so that the youths could learn to express and understand the ties among feelings, thoughts and actions. This will eventually lead to acknowledgment of depression and help work out its causes. This should help a client reach a stabilized emotional state. The child or adolescent will redevelop interest in and evidence of energy, activities and socialization that promote an elevated mood. The irritability in the client will be reduced and normal interaction with family and friends will be increased. The client will establish healthy eating and sleeping patterns. The client will develop coping and stress reducing skills. Each of the long term goals can be met with the use of developed short-term goals and interventions. For example, one of the first goals is to have the youth and counselor work together, have the youth begin to understand the dynamic relationship among thoughts, feelings, and behaviors, and the youth more appropriately express feelings. Several short-term goals will help accomplish this long-term goal. Goals and interventions need to be tied to depressive symptoms and a major goal always is to reduce or eliminate those symptoms. Chapter Two begins to illustrate this process for you.

CHAPTER 2
Short Term Goals
The Dynamic Role of Feelings, Thoughts, and Behaviors that Contribute to Depression

Short Term Goal 1: The counselor will build rapport with the client. This is the working together process.

The following are ways to build therapeutic alliance with a client. It is important to build a therapeutic alliance with all patients, but it is especially important when working with youths. Adolescents are going through many changes in their lives and one that is having recurrent thoughts of death, suicidal ideation, and suicidal attempts will need someone they can trust to talk with and work through these issues. There are many other ways to build therapeutic alliance. Here are a few ways to help get started.

Create an inviting environment for the client. The room should be decorated according to the age group you work with and should be a calming environment. Use calming colors like taupe, soft greens and blues. Pink is also a very calming color and is used often in prisons to control violent behaviors. Some colors can be too much of a good thing—like blue, it is calming, but sometimes too much can make a person depressed (http://www.christianwomentoday.com/home/color.html). Besides paying attention to color, all offices should be inviting.

As a school counselor, I made sure that seating was appropriate in that my chairs were arranged so that both a youth and I sat at the same level, facing each other, and that the walls were decorated with colorful posters on blue walls. As a mental health practitioner, a licensed professional clinical counselor (LPCC) and a licensed marriage and family therapist (LMFT), my office setting varied from a renovated barn to an adobe style office befitting the practice I owned in the Southwest. My private offices contained Two Gray Hills Indian rugs, pottery, fireplaces, and plenty of green plants. A fish tank added to a soothing environment along with a muted lamp lighting so that no overhead lights glared.

Playing various therapeutic games like *The Ungame* by Talicor involve children and adolescents in therapy without you asking and having them answer questions directly. This sets a stage of sharing where the counselor and client answer questions together and the focus seems to be on a game rather then on oneself. Players progress along a playing board as they answer questions such as "What are the four most important things in your life," and "What do you think life will be like in 100 years?" This non-competitive game can be a great icebreaker or a serious exchange of thoughts, feelings and ideas. This game will help you get to know your client and help him or her feel comfortable working with you (http://www.boardgames.com/ungame.html). I have had teenagers and children who do not want to be in therapy. They were either court ordered or brought in by their parents, a teacher, or an administrator who wanted a problem defined and an instant fix to problems they were having. They did not know what to expect with a school counselor or a mental health therapist and asking direct questions seemed to set them off or caused instant forgetfulness about their lives. "I don't know" or silence would greet any type of question and sometimes rude comments like, "I am not going to talk to any kind of a shrink " would be the first thing I heard. I found that a warm smile and a comment about how I would like to get to know them and allow them to know me a little went a long way to winning some cooperation and to building a therapeutic alliance.

Depending on what I knew about the background of the child from in take forms or discussions with significant others in their lives, I would allow them to choose from a well stocked room with toys, art supplies, puppets, dolls and other materials or I would suggest a specific course of play action. Kaduson and Schaefer (2000) provide an in-depth discussion of such cognitive behavior therapy playrooms and Hobday and Ollier (1999) discuss various settings for children and adolescents. The point is that working with a child or an adolescent is different than working with an adult and engaging that youth in a process that allows the focus of therapy to develop and that fosters a therapeutic relationship is important.

A mental health practitioner will definitely want to build rapport with youths by using Rogerian principles to develop an unconditional positive relationship (Corey, 2001). The therapist's role is to maintain and show empathetic understanding and unconditional positive regard. The therapist will utilize active listening skills of paraphrasing, clarifying, and summarization throughout the counseling process but especially in the beginning where the young person provides leads that will need to be investigated during the play process. This will allow the client to know that the therapist is genuinely listening and showing empathy toward the client.

For example, one serious case involved a fourteen-year-old patient with cardiomyopathy. This young boy played basketball with a vengeance until one day, he collapsed on the court and the doctor discovered his large, heavy heart that put him on a heart transplant list. His depression, anger, and irritability over his condition added to his physical burden. He felt that he had nothing to discuss since his basketball days and his life "was over." Rather than get into a question-answer frame with him in the first session, I put on a video taped college basketball game and asked him to explain the players' moves to me. As we focused on the game, he began to loosen up and discuss why he was upset. He said not being able to run and play was scarier than facing death. We began a journey that day that took us many places because he began to trust me and see that I cared about him, his family, and his desires.

Short-Term Goal 2: The counselor will refer the client, suspected of major depression, to a child psychiatrist for evaluation for medications.

In a truly depressed client, psychopharmacology as well as psychotherapy work well together. If a child psychiatrist determines that a young person needs medication, the counselor can best help by understanding and explaining how the medication works, how long it will take for the client to begin to see results, and what the side effects might be.

The client will need to cooperate with a referral to a physician to evaluate the need for psychotropic medication. A discussion of this needs to be directed primarily to the primary care-taker since he or she will be taking these steps and making these decisions.

Discuss with the parents the symptoms of depression and the role of medication. Preston et al. (2002) provides a quick reference table on page 84 for when to medicate for Depressive Disorders. The table is organized by events and their symptoms. When grief becomes clinical depression, the symptoms are: early morning awakening, serious weight loss, anhedonia, and agitation.

Paul Markovitz, M.D., Ph.D., (2002) states, "Antidepressants do not change the hardwiring. They simply dampen down the circuits to a point where many individuals can control their lives. Mood swings, somatic complaints, rage, irritability, binge eating, anxiety, and even black-white thinking are reduced significantly."

The counselor will need to encourage client to take medication as prescribed and one way to do this is by having them complete a medication log each day. A medication log helps client keep track of when and how often they take their prescribed medications. The therapist on a weekly basis can check a simple log like the one here. While examining the log, the counselor can help the young person identify possible side effects or problems that need to be reported to the physician.

The side effect checklists on previous pages are helpful to keep in a client's file and can be considered while checking on the medication log.

MEDICATION LOG

Name:

MONTH:

Date:	1	2	3	4	5	6	7	8	9	10	11	12	13	14	15
Dose 1															
Time															
Initial															
Dose 2															
Time															
Initial															

Date:	16	17	18	19	20	21	22	23	24	25	26	27	28	29	30
Dose 1															
Time															
Initial															
Dose 2															
Time															
Initial															

Helping young people stay on prescribed medications is very important and is something that both the caregiver and counselor can do to help a young person.

Short Term Goal 3: Teach the young person to identify feelings and then to connect their thoughts and feelings.

One of the things that happen to mental health practitioners in training is that that are taught two courses on theory, a basic theories course and then an advanced theories class, and one or two courses on techniques. Many times, there is little discussion about how to apply the theoretical orientation or techniques to specific client problems like depression. With Cognitive Behavior Therapy (CBT) recognized as a successful treatment for depression in youths, we can utilize step-by-step interventions to help depressed young people. One of the first theorists to discuss Cognitive Behavior Therapy was Dr. Albert Ellis, who first named his theory Rational Emotive Therapy (RET), then changed the name to Rational Emotive Behavior Therapy (REBT). Based on the work of Albert Ellis, founder of the Institute for Rational-Emotive Therapy in New York, RET is a counseling intervention generally based on the assumption that emotional problems result from faulty thinking about events rather than from events themselves. As such, it involves a cognitive-emotive-behavioral system. This idea is illustrated by the A-B-C-D-E theory of emotional disturbance, where A is an activating event, B are beliefs about the event, and C is the emotional and behavioral consequence.

A	B	C	D	E
Activating Event	**Beliefs**	**Consequence**	**Disputing**	**Effect of Disputes**

Many people feel that activating events cause consequences. However, RET thinking holds that beliefs about the event intervene and are critical in determining consequences.

Ellis' theory is based on an A-B-C-D-E paradigm:

A = Activating Event. Things happen in life, and whenever something happens a person responds.

B = Beliefs about the activating event. Ellis claims that whenever something happens, a person forms a belief about the event and the belief formed causes the person to feel, act, and think either in a rational manner or an irrational manner.

Rational beliefs cause a person to feel the way s/he would like to feel and to behavior responsibly. Irrational beliefs cause people to feel bad, sad, depressed, etc. and to behave in an irresponsible manner. Irrational beliefs contain elements of: childish demandingness, critical evaluation of self and/or others, and problematic thinking. Problematic thinking includes forms of thinking like:

- *Shouldistic thinking*—"People should treat me the way I want to be treated." "I should get what I want out of life with little or no hassle." "People should be . . ."

- *Musterbation*—"I must be treated with respect and kindness." "I must do well in all of my endeavors."

- *Awfulizing*—"It is awful and terrible that things aren't going my way." "This is so awful that things will never be better."

- *I-Can't-Stand-It-Itis*—"You make me so mad that I can't stand it any more."

- *Wormhood*—"You are such a worm for doing what you did that you should be severely blamed and punished." "I am so bad that I should be damned and I don't deserve anything from life."

C = Consequences—affective, behavioral, and cognitive.

Rational beliefs cause one to feel like they want to feel or to feel appropriately, to behave rationally and responsibly and to think about the situation in a reasonable manner while irrational beliefs cause one to be depressed, sad, angry, or upset, to behave irrationally and irresponsibly, and to think about the situation in an unreasonable manner. To know if one is thinking reasonably, one asks:

1. Is this thought based on fact?

2. Does this thought help me reach my goals?

3. Does this thought produce conflict with others?

4. Does this thought help me feel the way I want to feel?

5. Does this thought help me protect my life and health?

D = Disputing. This is the process where the counselor helps the client learn to dispute irrational thoughts. Counselors must learn to dispute the basic irrational thoughts that clients have and should practice doing that before using REBT.

E = Effect of disputing where clients have changed their feelings, actions, and thoughts by changing their thinking.

Many people feel that activating events cause consequences. However, RET thinking holds that beliefs about the event intervene and are critical in determining consequences. If beliefs are rational, they result in moderate emotions that enable people to act constructively and achieve their goals. In contrast, irrational beliefs lead to disturbed emotions such as anger, anxiety, or depression, thus making goal attainment difficult.

The core construct of RET is that emotional upset stems from three major irrational beliefs.

1. I must do well and win approval for my performances, or else I rate as a rotten person.

2. Others must treat me considerately and kindly in precisely the way I want them to treat -me; if they don't, society and the universe should severely blame, damn, and punish them for their inconsiderateness.

3. Conditions under which I live must be arranged so that I get practically everything I want comfortably, quickly, and easily, and get virtually nothing that I don't want. (Ellis, 1980, pp. 5–7).

These irrational beliefs result in some very nonproductive feelings and attitudes.

1. *Worthlessness* ("I am a worthless person if I don't do as well and win as much approval as I must.")

2. *Awfulizing* ("It is awful, terrible, or horrible that I am not doing as I must.")

3. *I-can't-stand-it-itis* ("I can't stand, can't bear the things that are happening to me that must not happen!") (Ellis, 1980, p. 8)

4. The *"must"* that characterizes these feelings and attitudes translates into the following kinds of statements, easily recognizable to anyone who works with adolescents. It would be awful if my peers didn't like me; I shouldn't make mistakes, especially social mistakes; It's my parents' fault I'm so miserable; I can't help it, that's just the way I am and I guess I'll always be this way; The world should be fair and just; It's awful when things do not go my way; It's better to avoid challenges than risk failure; I must conform to my peers; I can't stand to be criticized; Others should always be responsible." (Waters, 1981, p. 6)

Once such irrational beliefs are identified, the D and E of the A-B-C paradigm become operative. *Disputing* (D) means challenging irrational beliefs by questioning assumptions about the event. As disputing occurs and rational beliefs replace irrational ones, more moderate *emotions* (E) result.

In 1970, the Institute for Rational Living opened The Living School, a private grade school in New York. The purpose of this school was to present RET concepts in addition to the typical elementary-level curriculum. During the course of the school's operation, it became evident that teachers could successfully help children improve their emotional health. REBT was used extensively with children and adolescents, either on an individual basis, in the classroom, or in small-group counseling sessions.

There are several reasons Cognitive Behavioral Therapy (CBT) works with youths. First, it is educative in nature, its goal being to help people help themselves by teaching them positive mental health concepts. More importantly, in teaching youths about the core irrational beliefs and attempts to modify those beliefs relate to many of the basic problems faced by young people today: equating self-worth with performance and therefore never feeling good about oneself; awfulizing about events, then reacting in self-defeating ways (for example, by abusing alcohol or drugs); over-generalizing and losing perspective on problems, then reacting impulsively (perhaps even by committing suicide). In addition, many young people seem to be caught up in the irrational attitude that things should come easily and this perspective results in impatience about having to work hard and set long-term goals. Finally, unless young people are taught to change these negative feelings by changing their thoughts, efforts at prevention or remediation will be superficial. A central goal of RET and CBT is to help people successfully alter these thoughts.

As noted by Bernard and Joyce (1984), the goal of preventative mental health programs is to facilitate the social and emotional growth of children by developing interpersonal relationship skills, enhancing self-esteem, improving problem-solving and decision-making strategies, developing a flexible outlook on life, acquiring a personal value system, and learning communication skills. REBT has morphed into CBT and can be used successfully to intervene with youngsters who are having specific mood disorder problems. There are many elements to Cognitive Behavior Therapy that can be used with children and adolescents who have mood disorders. We will discuss more about Cognitive Behavior Therapy as we move through interventions in a step-by-step manner. The first step has to do with emotions.

In the U.S. society, parents and caregivers often socialize boys and girls differently. If a little girl falls down and scrapes her knee, she is often cuddled, told to cry, and given permission to express a full range of hurt feelings. However, if a little boy falls, he is often told to suck it up, to act tough, and in essence, he is instructed to not feel. Often boys grow up believing that anger and tough feelings are the only ones that are acceptable while girls are encouraged to be more expressive. In some families, children face abuse and indifference and learn not to share feelings. In depression, feelings are often turned inward. With some young people and adolescents, there is a need to teach a child to recognize and understand feelings. Many interventions are designed to do this.

For all youths, a counselor will need to explain that feelings are neither right nor wrong; they just are. For very young children, a therapist can work with the child and teach about feelings by using magazines and child safe scissors. I like to use magazine pictures because they picture real life pictures of people instead of cartoon or balloon faces. I ask the child to cut out some pictures of different people and I do the same thing. As the child becomes involved in the counseling activity, I begin discussing how different people feel different things in their lives. I will take a picture of someone smiling and talk about the word, happy, and show the child a smiling person. I talk about the sign or cues that help me understand that this person looks happy. Then I will ask the child to find a picture of a happy person he or she can cut out. When the child finds that image, I glue it to a piece of paper and write the word, happy. Then with the child, I will go over the cues or signs that indicate that this person appears to be happy.

With young children, I first concentrate on five words, happy, sad, scared, tired, and mad. Each time, I have them find the pictures, I help them glue them to a piece of paper, we discuss the cues or signs that the person is sad, scared, mad, or tired. When we have all five words covered, I begin to role model by discussing the times I have been happy, sad, scared, tired, and mad. Then I ask the child to pick a picture and talk about a time or a situation when she or he might have felt that way. The more involved I can become with the child, the more I know I can reach the child. If the child is able, have him or her glue the pictures and write the words on the paper. The next page provides you with complete directions for this exercise and the next few pages after that will give you other worksheets (appropriate for different ages and abilities of young people) that you can use to teach young people how to identify their feelings.

Worksheet for Identifying Feelings

Directions:

1. Take two pieces of paper, two pairs of scissors, glue, and several magazines.

2. The counselor will give the child one piece of paper, one pair of scissors, some glue and some magazines.

3. The counselor keeps the other set, tells the child that s/he is going to find a picture of someone who is happy, cut out the picture and glue it to the paper.

4. After completing the activity, the counselor encourages the child to do the same thing.

5. After both have the pictures glued to the paper, the counselor writes the word, happy, by the pictures on both pieces of paper (if the child knows how to write the word, s/he will be instructed to do so.

6. Then the counselor talks a little about the expressions on the face, the posture of the person in his picture, the activity of the person, and any indicators that show the person pictured is happy.

7. The counselor then asks the child to point out happiness indicators on the child's picture.

8. Then the counselor finds a person who depicts sad, then scared, tired, and mad and perhaps other emotions and follows the same procedure.

9. Just working on the pictures is enough for one session with a child.

10. In the next session, the counselor would pull the pictures from the child's file, go over them in quick review and then take the happy picture.

11. The counselor would disclose a short story about the last time s/he was happy and then encourage the child to tell a similar story.

12. The counselor would do this with each emotion discussed.

Worksheet for Identifying Feelings

Directions:

Create a collage. Obtain a poster board 24 inches by 36 inches. Look in magazines/newspapers and cut out words, phrases, and other pictures that reflect your feelings about anything you would like to discuss. Arrange the pictures and words/phrases and secure them on the poster board in any way you feel best expresses your feelings. When you have completed your collage, you and I will work together to answer the following questions:

1. Explain briefly the pictures you chose and which two have the greatest significance for you.

2. Explain the reasons for the words/phrases you chose.

3. Looking over the collage you've created, what does it say to you about your feelings?

4. Do the pictures bring back any of the following feelings? (Circle any that apply.)

Anger	Guilt	Disappointment	Regret
Hurt	Worry	Abandonment	Rejection
Happy	Fun	Fear	Joy
Love	Peace	Satisfaction	Empowerment
Other: _____		Other: _____	

    Explain:

Labeling Emotions: Work with Young Children

Directions

Give a young child marking pens and paper with three evenly spaced boxes (so that writing can be fitted in above and below the pictures) and ask young children to draw three different faces (Happy, Sad, Angry). Then start with the happy picture and ask the child what makes them feel happy. (Ask younger children *when* they feel happy). Write down what the child says around the picture.

Happy Face

Sad Face

Angry Face

Letter Writing to Express Feelings

Directions:

Sometimes it is difficult to talk straight out to a counselor. I want you to write a letter to me discussing anything you might want to talk about. This can be a way to help identify and express your thoughts and feelings. This is especially true when you need to work through your feelings and understand your thinking about something. In this homework assignment, you are asked to write a letter to me about anything you want to help you identify and express your own feelings. You will give this letter to me at the beginning of our next session.

These are the steps you need to follow:

- First, find a quiet or relaxing place where you can write the letter. This will help you concentrate on writing down your thoughts and feelings without distractions. Perhaps you can write the letter in a quiet room in your house, at the library, or in a favorite outdoor place.

- Respond to the following questions designed to help you organize your thoughts and feelings before you begin to actually write the letter. You may find that some of these questions do not apply to you; therefore, leave those items blank. Space is also provided for you to express any additional thoughts or feelings that you may want to at this stage in the assignment. You can decide later as to whether you want to include these thoughts in your final letter.

1. What thoughts and feelings have you been experiencing?

2. What are some of the positive things in your life right now?

3. What are some of the hurts, problems, or disappointments in your life right now?

4. If something has not gone well for you, what, if anything, do you wish you could have said or done?

5. What mostly affects your present life?

6. Are you sorry about anything that has happened in your life? Describe.

7. Has your life changed any recently? Describe.

8. What are some of the important events that have occurred in your life?

9. What do you think is the most important thing that we can work on together?

10. How do you feel about coming to counseling?

Recognizing My Feelings

(Adaptation of Bisignano & McElmurry, 1987)

Directions:

This chart will help you recognize your feelings and help you understand the degree to which you experience each.

Check the appropriate box.

	Usually	Often	Sometimes	Seldom	Never
1. I feel happy					
2. I feel sad					
3. I feel lonely					
4. I feel accepted					
5. I feel bored					
6. I feel afraid					
7. I feel angry					
8. I feel peaceful					
9. I feel loved					
10. I feel hopeful					
11. I feel irritated					
12. I feel argumentative					
13. I feel like crying					
14. I feel like I don't care					
15. I feel like I can't sleep					
16. I feel disorganized					
17. I feel sick					
18. I feel stupid					
19. I feel like others are watching me					

Feelings Checklist

(Adapted from Riethmayer, 1993)

Directions:

In order to allow your feelings to help you know what you need, this week put a check by all of the feelings that you remember feeling that day. Remember, feelings are clues and signal about what's wrong or what we need to know. They are there to help you—if you learn to use them correctly. Begin to learn to name a feeling when you are having it.

Practice This Week With This Daily Checklist

Feeling	Monday	Tuesday	Wednesday	Thursday	Friday	Saturday	Sunday
Anger							
Sad							
Guilty							
Lonely							
Embarrassed							
Happy							
Afraid							
Nervous							
Disappointed							
Hate							
Frustrated							
Disgusted							
Love							
Caring							
Sure							
Jealous							
Excited							
Bored							
Confused							
Numb							
Hurt							
Calm							
Safe							
Scared							
Playful							
Shy							
Really Sad							
Ashamed							
Worried							
Panicked							
Abandoned							

Other Resources for Teaching Children to Identify Feelings

For grade school children, Auger (2005) describes three activities a counselor and a child can work through together. In Emotional Vocabulary, a set of index cards is created, each with the name of an emotion. The cards are placed face-down in front of the students, who take turns picking a card. Upon picking a card, the students read the emotion, state what it feels like, and give an example of a time they experienced the emotion.

The Emotional Pie technique simply consists of having students draw a large circle on a piece of paper, then divide the resulting pie into segments based on how often they have experienced particular feelings in the past day or week. School counselors working with younger students can ask them to divide their pie based on how much they had experienced the basic emotions of happy, sad, mad, and afraid. Older students can be provided with a more extensive list of feelings, or be allowed to select their own feeling words.

The Emotional Thermometer is another simple technique in which the school counselor draws a large thermometer on a board or a large piece of paper, and then asks the students to rate the emotional intensity of various situations they have experienced. The intent of this technique is to teach children that the strength of emotions varies depending on the situation.

Connecting Feelings and Thoughts

A major goal of Cognitive Behavior Therapy is to teach youths that feelings are the results of thoughts that they have. This step in CBT is very important. Many people, including adults fail to make this connection and find it easy to blame others for their feelings and actions rather than take personal responsibility for the way they think or what they do. All of us have heard someone say, "He makes me so mad!" or "She makes me so depressed!" Teaching any person that she or he is responsible for his or her own feelings is important. A strong tenet of CBT is that no one can make you feel mad, depressed, angry, or upset. A person can do something we do not like and we can choose to react in a variety of ways. Remember that our short term goal is *Teach the young person to identify feeling and then to connect their thoughts and feelings.* The next exercise is to teach a young person that he or she is responsible for his or her own feelings.

Others Are Not Responsible for Our Feelings

Directions:

- Provide the client with a pen and a chart on paper. The chart should look like this:

Situation	Feelings	Thoughts

- Then begin a discussion. Discuss what it means to be disappointed. Provide a self-disclosed example and write it out on the chart with the client watching. Example:

Situation	Feelings	Thoughts
I wanted cake for dessert and there was nothing for dessert.	I felt irritated.	I thought my husband (wife) should have made something for dessert.

- Ask the youth to make a list of the last three times s/he was disappointed, to explain how s/he reacted to the disappointment (cried, yelled, argued, blamed, etc.), how s/he felt, and what s/he thought. Concentrate on the thoughts and feelings. Write the three situations on a chart; if possible have the youth write this himself or herself.

Situation 1	Feelings	Thoughts
Situation 2	**Feelings**	**Thoughts**
Situation 3	**Feelings**	**Thoughts**

- Ask the client to identify who they think is to blame for his or her unhappiness or disappointment in each situation.

- Take the first situation and illustrate that unhappy feelings come from our thoughts. For example, if the client is disappointed that he or she was not able to sit by a friend at lunch, s/he would likely be thinking and saying to herself or himself something like:

  "No one likes me."

  "That no good Fred. He should have left a spot for me."

  "I am pretty mad right now."

- Discuss the fact that not everyone would think and feel the way the client thinks and feels. For example, another student might think and say:

  "It's too bad I didn't ask Fred to save me a seat."

  "I need to tell Fred that I would like to sit next to him next time."

  "I didn't get what I wanted so I will have to figure out what to do next time."

- Ask the child to decide how s/he would have felt after saying the last things to herself or himself.

- Go through all three situations the client has provided and have the child develop different statements and discuss the different feelings in relation to less critical, less demanding, and less childish (all elements of irrational thinking). This is also a good time to point out that sometimes our thoughts contain problematic thinking and this is a time to begin to dispute such thinking.

  Remember that problematic thinking includes forms of thinking like:

  Shouldistic thinking—"People should treat me the way I want to be treated." "I should get what I want out of life with little or no hassle." "People should be . . ."

  Musterbation—"I must be treated with respect and kindness." "I must do well in all of my endeavors."

  Awfulizing—"It is awful and terrible that things aren't going my way." "This is so awful that things will never be better."

  I-Can't-Stand-It-Itis—"You make me so mad that I can't stand it any more."

  Wormhood—"You are such a worm for doing what you did that you should be severely blamed and punished." "I am so bad that I should be damned and I don't deserve anything from life."

- You would ask the child who makes the statement, "No one likes me" to provide the evidence that no one likes him or her and you would dispute the thought by helping the child provide evidence that indeed someone does like him or her.

- You would take the statement, "That no good Fred. He should have left a spot for me," and discuss the fact that no one always gets what s/he wants in life and although it would have been nice if the student had been able to sit next to Fred, there is no rhyme, reason, or rule about who *should* get to do that.

- You would take the statement, "I'm pretty mad right now" and explain to the child that s/he is the one deciding to be mad and that other statements would make them feel differently.

The Thought Record and the Daily Mood Log

To tie up the links between thoughts and feelings and actions, cognitive behavior therapists use a tool called the thought record. This has a long history in the mental health field. Several important theories of depression, including Beck's (1976) cognitive theory, Seligman's (Abramson, Selignian, & Teasdale, 1978) learned helplessness theory and Abramson and colleagues' (e.g., Abramson, Metalsky, & Alloy, 1989) hopelessness theory state that negative mood and maladaptive behaviors are caused by negative, maladaptive, irrational, distorted cognitions. Beck termed these cognitions "automatic thoughts" because they arise automatically, without effort or intention. Beck's theory in particular states very explicitly that to treat negative mood and maladaptive behaviors, the therapist needs to change the negative cognitions that cause them (Beck, Rush, Shaw, & Emery 1979).

Important theories of depression that have been around for over thirty years state that negative mood and maladaptive behaviors are caused by negative, maladaptive, irrational, distorted cognitions. This fits Albert Ellis's Rational Emotive Therapy conceptual framework and also the work on depression by Beck (1976). Beck termed these cognitions "automatic thoughts" because they arise automatically, without effort or intention. Beck's theory, in particular, states very explicitly that to treat negative mood and maladaptive behaviors, the therapist needs to change the negative cognitions that cause them. In order to treat child and adolescent depression, it will be very important to tie thoughts, feelings, and behavior together in a way that a young person can understand that his or her thinking is creating a negative mood state and creating depression. This has to be done in such a way that the child or teenager does not fall into guilty feelings for having such thoughts or that others do not enter "the blame the victim game."

A thought record looks like this:

Date	Situation (event, memory, attempt to do something)	Behaviors	Emotions	Thoughts	Consequence

Ideally, a counselor would make copies of the thought record, keep one and hand one to any client who knows how to write. For young children, the counselor will need to determine how the child thinks and would use the thought record after a play therapy session, after playing a game with the client, or after the use of some intervention or technique that provides the counselor with evidence of the child's thinking.

Notice that the Thought Record mirrors the central components of CBT theory: It has columns for a counselor to record the date of a specific incident, the situation (the external event that activates automatic thinking or irrational thinking that triggers cognitions, moods, and behaviors. Once the counselor can determine the thinking behind the feelings and actions of a client, s/he can help plan interventions that would lead to adaptive, reasonable, realistic cognitions and behavioral action plans that serve as healthy, productive, adaptive responses to the distorted cognitions. The Thought Record then can be used to teach the cognitive model and to promote cognitive-behavioral change.

The Thought Record is a tool children and adolescents can use to arrive at a different way to view a problematic situation that would allow them to feel and function better. There are three ways a counselor can use the thought record.

First, the counselor can determine the usefulness of the client's cognitions in the problematic situation. The counselor can ask the client the following: Does this way of thinking about the situation help you? Does it cause you to feel the way you want to feel? Does this way of thinking help you get what you want? How does it cause you to function? Is there another way of thinking about this situation that would help you feel better and that would create a different outcome in your life?

Second, the counselor can use a Thought Record to identify cognitive distortions. Aaron Beck, David Burns, and others (Beck et al., 1979; Burns, 1999) identified and named the typical cognitive distortions that depressed patients make. Often clients feel better by simply identifying the distortions in their thinking.

Third, the counselor can use a Thought Record by identifying the thinking distortion and help the client generate responses to his or her distorted thoughts. For example, noticing that the thought "No one likes me" involves overgeneralization can help the patient generate a good response to it (e.g., "just because Fred did not sit by me at lunch, this does not mean that no one likes me.").

To make effective use of the Thought Record, counselors should follow two guidelines: Never lecture and be careful with the use of questions and focus on concrete, specific situations. Questions should help the youth think about something in a new way. Most youths are not receptive to other peoples' ideas about how they "should" think about things. In training counselors, I cannot tell you how many times I have witnessed a new counselor working with a child in a school setting with this scenario.

The counselor ends up lecturing the child to change the behavior without first going through the necessary steps of developing a therapeutic relationship. The counselor should ascertain the child's view of the situation and the child's thought processes. A goal is to help the child see where his or her thinking created a negative outcome in the situation and help the child develop a new view of the situation. Eventually the counselor will help the child develop a new way of thinking and being in future situations.

The new counselor more often than not, zooms in on the child and demands that the child not fight. The counselor lectures the child and tells him that he is sure that the child knows other ways of dealing with conflict. The counselor then asks the child what s/he could do instead of fighting. Often the child will recite a litany of "acceptable behaviors." The child states that he could take a deep breath, he could tell a teacher on duty about the situation before fighting, or he could simply walk away.

Confident, that he has done a good job, the new counselor sends the child on his way with a pat on the back and a few minutes later, the child gets into a fight once again. In this scenario, the counselor turned into another adult telling a child what he should do. Children are not stupid. They often know what they should say to appease an adult. The counselor's mistake was in using an approach that did not utilize good counseling skills, have the child WORK THROUGH the situation in a personally meaningful manner, or allow the child to see how his thinking created an unfortunate result which not did help him in life in an appropriate way.

Productive therapeutic work results from a focus on a specific, concrete situation that is used in the form of a written record. If the child or teenager focuses on an actual concrete event, he or she is more likely to remember, and even begin to experience again, the thoughts and feelings he or she experienced in that situation. This information is needed to understand the youth's distress and to work to alleviate it. In addition, general discussions not tied to a specific situation tend to become dry, sterile, and intellectual debates that are devoid of emotional charge; these types of discussions are rarely productive. The focus on a specific situation activates the emotional charge necessary for therapeutic change. The written record, especially aligned with another tool in the CBT arsenal, the Schema Change Record, will show a child or teenager that there can be positive change. Often depressed youths believe that nothing ever changes. Young people, just like adult clients, will often take two steps forward and then a step backward. In other words, they will do well for awhile, but slip back into old, defeated patterns. That is why constant work and sessions with the youth is important.

Patients who suffer from depression often lose interest in people and activities around them. The following interventions are designed to help an adolescent patient examine her or his reasons for this and take steps to improve.

Daily Mood Log:

Beginning with a Daily Mood Log encourages the youth to identify her automatic thoughts (those that occur without effort) when she thinks about doing something she knows would be good for her but that she is resisting or when she decides to do nothing. She will be taught to look for distortions (irrational thinking) and to replace those distortions with more rational responses.

First the counselor exposes the patient to Dr. David Burns' list of Cognitive Distortions. Notice these are very similar to the distortions first described by Albert Ellis in an earlier part of this book. They discuss some of the patient's automatic thoughts and distortions.

Following is Burns' "Checklist of Cognitive Distortions."

1. **All-or-nothing thinking:** Looking at things in absolute, black-and-white categories.

2. **Overgeneralization:** Viewing a negative event as a never-ending pattern of defeat.

3. **Mental filter:** Dwelling on the negatives and ignoring the positives.

4. **Discounting the positives:** Insisting that accomplishments or positive qualities "don't count."

5. **Jumping to conclusions:** (A) Mind reading – assuming that people are reacting negatively to you when there's no evidence for this; (B) Fortune-telling – Arbitrarily predicting that things will turn out badly.

6. **Magnification or minimization:** Blowing things way up out of proportion or shrinking their importance inappropriately.

7. **Emotional reasoning:** Reasoning from how you feel: "I feel like an idiot, so I really must be one."

8. **"Should statements":** Criticizing yourself or other people with "shoulds" or "shouldn'ts."

9. **Labeling:** Identifying shortcomings. Instead of saying, "I made a mistake," you tell yourself, "I'm a loser."

10. **Personalization and blame:** Blaming yourself for something you weren't entirely responsible for, or blaming other people and overlooking ways that your own attitudes and behavior might contribute to the problem.

The "Daily Mood Log" is a simple three-column grid. Columns are labeled "Automatic Thoughts," "Distortions," and "Rational Responses" respectively. After entering automatic thoughts the client also rates her belief in each one using a scale of 0–100 (Burns, 1999).

Automatic Thoughts	Distortions	Rational Responses
I failed a quiz in science. I am no good. I will never pass this class.	Labeling Magnification Blame	I did not do as well as I would have liked on the quiz. Next time I will need to study so that I can do better

The patient is given the Daily Mood Log as a homework assignment. She is asked to record her thoughts each time she finds herself "down in the dumps" about an activity she is doing or anticipating. When the patient returns for the next session, she and the counselor examine the log. They discuss her automatic thoughts and distortions one at a time. The counselor uses Socratic questioning to guide the patient in replacing the distortions with rational responses. (Socratic questioning is a line of questioning meant to lead the client into discovering new ways of thinking about the subject.) This continues from session to session with the counselor and patient reviewing older logs and evaluating progress. Fewer distortions or lower ratings for those distortions signal improvement. As clients recognize erroneous thinking, they often change behavior. In this case the patient should begin to report more enjoyment and, as a result, more participation in activities. Once the Mood Log has been established, the counselor is ready to implement the Thought Record.

Thought Record:

As it has been previously mentioned, it is the belief of cognitive therapists that, "negative mood and maladaptive behaviors are caused by negative, maladaptive, irrational, distorted cognitions." (Abramson, Metalsky, & Alloy, 1989). This is the basis for the thought record. Some examples of irrational, distorted cognitions are listed above in Burns' checklist and in the writing of Albert Ellis.

47

The therapist uses the Thought Record to help the patient examine the usefulness of her cognitions, identify cognitive distortions (which often helps a patient feel better by itself), and analyze in detail the evidence supporting and not supporting a distortion. The therapist focuses on a single concrete situation. Often when a child or adolescent comes into a counseling session, the young person will have a dozen things running through his or her mind. This client will have a need to tell you several things at one time. In order to focus the client and zoom in on one situation, the thought record may be necessary. In actuality, a counselor and a client can only deal with one thing at a time. If a client of any age just keeps on talking, more times than not, this person will talk mostly about someone else—how that person made them feel, how that person caused them to do something, and how everything is someone else's fault. To discourage this type of dialogue and irresponsibility, the thought record is useful.

After clearly writing down the thoughts, the consequences of the distorted thinking (feelings, actions, and further thinking), the counselor returns to the place in the Thought Record where the original distorted thought appeared and uses Socratic questioning to guide the client to healthier responses. Socratic questioning is recommended rather than directives because it gives the patient ownership, and therefore, more investment in the outcome.

Thought Record

Date	Situation (event, memory, attempt to do something)	Behaviors	Emotions	Thoughts
7-1-05	I failed a quiz in science	Threw my book down	Felt depressed and lousy	I am no good. I will never pass this class.
7-1-05	Got into a fight with my mother over the clothes I wanted to wear. She objected to the outfit.	Yelled back at my mother.	Felt mad and upset.	I should get to wear whatever I want to wear. I should do what I want.

Cognitive Thinking Report

(Adapted from Vorrath & Brendtro, 1985)

Name: _____ Date: _____

1. **Situation:** This is not a report of thinking but describes the situation where the thinking took place. This part of the Thinking Report should be brief and objective—stating the facts of the situation and including your behavior during that situation.

   _____

   _____

   _____

   _____

   _____

   _____

   _____

   _____

2. **Thoughts:** This is a list of all the thoughts you can remember having during the given situation or moment of time. After listing, label each thought in the order they occurred. A Thinking Report presents your thoughts as pure, objective information. Criticism of the thinking or excuses for the thinking is not appropriate in a Thinking Report.

   _____

   _____

   _____

   _____

   _____

   _____

   _____

   _____

   _____

3. **Feelings:** This is a list of all the feelings you can remember having during the given situation or moment of time. Similar to the Thoughts section, the feelings are presented as pure, objective information.

_____

_____

_____

_____

_____

_____

_____

_____

_____

4. **Attitudes/Beliefs:** This is a description of the more basic level of your thinking—your "background thinking." We don't make a technical distinction between attitudes and beliefs but use whichever term seems most appropriate in a given context. Attitudes and beliefs can be defined as a general way of thinking about a person or a situation or about the way you think things should be OR attitudes and beliefs can be defined as "the thinking behind our particular thoughts and feelings."

Attitude = mental state-how you present yourself; a result of how you think or feel; with you all the time.

Belief = Opinions/expectations that we believe to be true—learned from family or experiences.

_____

_____

_____

_____

_____

_____

_____

_____

_____

5. Explain why these are Key Thoughts and why they were Critical to the Situation.

_____

_____

_____

_____

_____

_____

_____

_____

_____

_____

6. **Triggering Event:** What started you thinking these Key Thoughts?

_____

_____

_____

_____

_____

_____

_____

_____

_____

7. My dispute to help overcome my reluctance to avoid people, places, or activities is:

_____

_____

_____

_____

_____

_____

_____

The Positive Data Log

One main cognitive behavior therapy technique is the use of a tool to change the young person's thinking. Several thought change methods have been developed, including continuum methods (Padesky, 1994), the historical test of schema (Young, 1990), the core belief worksheet (J. S. Beck, 1995), and the Positive Data Log (Padesky, 1994). A Positive Data Log is a log of evidence in support of an individual's positive or balancing schema.

Thought change methods have been called many things in the history of cognitive therapy, but we will use the idea of a Positive Data Log to show a young person how to change his or her thoughts. One person who contributed greatly to this idea was Aaron Beck way back in 1976. Beck called thoughts "schemes" much like Jean Piaget did when he was explaining the way children began to develop thought patterns in life. Schemas are deep cognitive structures that enable an individual to interpret his or her experiences in a meaningful way (Beck, 1976).

In Beck's cognitive theory, depressed patients have distorted, negative schema that when activated by life events give rise to negative automatic thoughts (e.g., "I can't do this"), problematic moods (e.g., depression), and maladaptive behaviors (e.g., procrastination). According to the cognitive theory if a patient experiences a symptom remission but retains pathological schema, he or she is vulnerable to relapse. Therefore, cognitive therapists believe it is important to work in therapy to change negative, pathological schema.

With young people, you will refer to the client's Thought Record and indicate to the young person that his or her thoughts (schemas) appeared when s/he was involved in a situation. Ellis called the situation an "Activating Event" and explained that activating events caused people to move into a string of thoughts that Beck and Burns called automatic thoughts. Ellis called the automatic thoughts beliefs. You have the young person write down his or her thought(s) in the appropriate space below. Then you have them write down the consequence(s) of their thinking. Then you move to the next box and enter information for alternative positive thoughts or schemas.

Positive Data Log

Instructions:

Describe your maladaptive, negative schema and alternative positive schema in the space provided. Then write down each piece of evidence that shows the consequences of your thinking and next write down your positive thoughts and list evidence of what will happen with your new way of thinking. Be as specific as possible. For example, rather than writing "I got mad," write "Mom didn't like my outfit and we got into a fight." Remember, you are to write down all your thoughts and then develop an alternative, positive way of thinking and what you think will happen, regardless of how small or insignificant you might think it is.

Negative thoughts (schemas):

_____

_____

_____

Alternative schema or thought(s):

_____

_____

_____

Date and time	Consequence of the negative thought or schema

Date and time	What might happen with my changed thoughts

Next, you challenge the youth to try the changed thinking and keep a record of actually what did happen. That record would look like this:

Date and time	Evidence of alternative positive schema

Example:

Negative thoughts (schemas):

I thought that I should be able to wear what I wanted to wear and that I should be able to do exactly

what I want to do whenever I want.

Alternative schema or thought(s):

Although it would be nice to get what I want when I want it, that is not the way the real world works.

My mother does care about me and the way I look. I will discuss with her the objections she has about

my dress and explain why I chose the outfit that I did.

Date and time	Consequence of the negative thought or schema
7-1-05	*Yelled at my mother. Got slapped. Felt angry and upset.*

Date and time	What might happen with my changed thoughts
7-5-05	*Might have a discussion instead of a fight. Might have Mom approve of what I wear or come up with a compromise.*

Next, you challenge the youth to try the changed thinking and keep a record of actually what did happen. That record would look like this:

Date and time	Evidence of alternative positive schema
7-10-05	*Mom and I discussed the fight we had and decided that I would pick out three outfits each night and she would discuss with me her thoughts instead of fighting and yelling. She promised to listen to my reasons for wanting to dress the way I want. Didn't get mad, have a fight, or feel angry.*

While the Positive Data Log will work with highly verbal children and older youths, sometimes, other interventions work with others. Now we are ready to move on to the main symptoms of depression exhibited by youths and discuss interventions that will work to alleviate or reduce those symptoms based on the scientific models suggested for treatment of the mood disorder.

CHAPTER 3
Counseling Interventions
Reducing the Symptoms of Depression

The focus of this chapter is on reducing or eliminating symptoms related to depression by using interventions that are consistent with best practice guidelines while working with children and adolescents. Teaching the cognitive model from Chapter Two begins a process that in itself will set a young person on the road to recovery. In some settings like school settings, reducing symptoms will help a young person gain some control of his or her life and will help the child concentrate on academic achievement, social skills, and home life. With only 5% of children receiving adequate mental health care in the United States, mental health workers, including school counselors, can use these interventions that require only minutes of time when practiced individually to help a child or an adolescent function better when they are depressed. Following the model completely, teaching the skills from cognitive behavior therapy in an organized consistent model would be the best use of this book, but even if the interventions are used as tools in a singular manner to help youths, they provide value.

Short Term Goal 1: Reduce a Sad/Depressed Mood Expressed by Feelings of Irritability

Young people need to learn that they can control their own sense of irritability. The following counseling interventions will help a young person learn this.

I Can Control Myself

Directions:

You can learn to manage your irritability and keep it under control even if others around you are irritating you. Remind yourself that you are a person who has choices and one choice you have is to control your own behavior.

Write down this fact:

"I can manage my own irritability any time I choose."

Now stand up and say, *"I can manage my own irritability any time I choose."*

Now whisper and say, *"I can manage my own irritability any time I choose."*

Stand on one foot and say, *"I can manage my own irritability any time I choose."*

In a squeaky voice say, *"I can manage my own irritability any time I choose."*

With your hands on your head say, *"I can manage my own irritability any time I choose."*

While making a funny face, say, *"I can manage my own irritability any time I choose."*

Sitting down say, *"I can manage my own irritability any time I choose."*

With your eyes closed say, *"I can manage my own irritability any time I choose."*

In a deep voice say, *"I can manage my own irritability any time I choose."*

In a singing voice say, *"I can manage my own irritability any time I choose."*

Lying on your back say, *"I can manage my own irritability any time I choose."*

Kneeling say, *"I can manage my own irritability any time I choose."*

What other ways you can think of to say this statement aloud? Write three down on the lines below.

_____

_____

_____

Now, for the next week, practice doing and saying these things whenever you begin to feel irritable. Take this paper with you so that you can remind yourself what to do when you feel irritable. I will check with you to see how you are doing with this problem.

Another exercise that can teach children that they are responsible for their own behavior and that they can direct their irritability in a safe and productive direction as they learn that their irritability is related to the way they think.

Safe Ways to Reduce Irritable Feelings

Directions:

- With pencils, markers, crayons, and a worksheet using I FEEL STATEMENTS, teach students to use "I feel" statements that will help them communicate clearly instead of feeling irritated.

- Tell the students: Using "I feel" statements can help you to let out your irritability safely. When you are irritable, express your feeling aloud by saying what you are feeling and why. If you use the "I feel" statement form to express yourself, you will be owning your feelings and not criticizing or blaming others. An "I feel" statement sounds like this: "I feel _____ when you _____ because _____."

- Then provide an example from your own life. "For example, when my children leave their rooms messy, I say to them: I feel hurt when you leave your rooms messy because it takes all of us in this family to keep the house clean and if you expect me to do all the work by myself, it is taking advantage of me."

- Now, tell me about a time you felt irritable with someone.

- Tell me how you could use an "I feel" statement to express your irritability.

- Draw pictures in the space on the next page of three people with whom you are often irritable. Think of the reasons you feel angry, and fill in the blanks in the "I feel" statements under the pictures.

I feel angry with _____ because: _____

_____

_____

Now fill in the blanks for this statement:

I _____
  (your feeling)

when you _____
  (situation)

because _____
  (reasons)

Drawing:

Young persons need to learn that their feelings of irritability or anger can best be managed at a low level before the feelings escalate. Use the following intervention to teach this.

Body Check—Manage

Directions:

Explain that irritability and anger is easier to manage when it is at a low level. If you notice your irritableness and identify why you feel it as soon as you begin to feel it, you will be able to find a safe way to manage it before it gets so big it explodes. Three steps to remember are . . .

1. Check your body

2. Identify why I feel irritable

3. Manage my anger safely

   Fill in the blanks below to show that you that you can check, identify, and manage irritability:

   1. How do you know that you are becoming irritable or angry? Mark any body changes that happen with you:

   When you become irritated or angry, several things begin to happen to your body:

   - Large amount of adrenaline pumped into the body to put us in a state of increased alertness and you will experience sweating, trembling and shaking.

   - Blood is redirected away from the extremities to the large muscles of the body and you may feel pins and needles and/or feel dizzy with cold hands and feet.

   - The heart starts working harder to move the blood to the large muscle groups as quickly as it can cause a racing heart where your heart actually beats faster.

   - There is an increase in respiratory rate to bring more oxygen into the body and you will breathe harder.

   - There is a release of sugar by the liver as an instant form of energy to make you want to do something like run or fight.

   - There will even be an increase in your metabolic rate to break down the sugar for energy to make you want to run or fight.

   - Your muscles will tense up.

Tell me what your body does by marking the following:

My body does the following things:

_____ sweat

_____ tremble

_____ shake

_____ feels like pins and needles

_____ feels dizzy

_____ cold hands and feet

_____ heart beats faster

_____ breathe harder

_____ moves me to run

_____ moves me to fight

2. Identify—I feel irritable because problem: _____

_____

_____

_____

3. I can manage my irritability safely by: _____

_____

_____

_____

Counselors can teach children to find a safe place to express irritability or anger.

Safety Zone

Directions:

You can create a place in your house or in your room that is specially reserved for letting out irritable feelings. This can make it easier for you to find safe ways to let your anger out. Whenever you feel filled with irritability, you can go directly to this place and let it out without hurting anyone or anything.

Pretend you are a designer who has been asked to create a "Safe Zone" for your house. Draw a picture of your house and show where you would put the Safe Zone. Then circle the things from the list below that you could do to get your feelings out in the space below. Add your own ideas. Choose things that would help you let your anger out safely. Draw these items into your picture.

Jump up and down	Tear up paper	Write a letter
Jump rope	Sing loudly	Draw with paper and crayons
Yell	Play a radio or stereo	Punch a bag
Throw pillows	Hammer something	

Young people need to learn that their thinking will create consequences and that there are outlets for irritability and anger that are safe and that there are outlets that create harm.

Consequences

Procedure:

When you express your irritability in safe ways, the results (the consequences) can be positive. But when you express your irritability in harmful ways, the consequences are usually negative.

Juan did not study for a test and thought to himself that he could get away with cheating. He cheated and got caught and now tells himself that he is mad because he can't go out for recess with the rest of the class.

What did Juan think? _____

_____

_____

What did Juan's thinking lead him to do? _____

_____

_____

What happened? _____

_____

_____

What caused Juan to become mad? _____

_____

_____

What could Juan say to himself other than saying to himself that it was okay to cheat and other than he is now angry? _____

_____

_____

When is the last time you made yourself irritable or angry? What could you tell yourself to have things come out differently? _____

_____

_____

Teach youths to channel pent up energy from irritability or anger into constructive activities.

Letting Feelings Out Constructively

You can safely let out irritability by channeling your frustrated energy into a productive activity. When you feel irritable energy building up inside, think of a way to use it up by doing something you enjoy or something that needs to be done.

Unscramble the last word in the phrases below to identify some ways to channel irritability energy productively.

Procedure:

Discuss with student how these things can help the student to cope with being irritable.

Clean my _____. Ormo

Brush my _____. Thete

Shovel _____. Nows

Rake _____. Sevela

Wash _____. Sthcloe

Walk my _____. Gdo

Take a _____. Athb

Plant a _____. Eret

Clean out my _____. Slecto

Play with my _____. Dgo

Teach young people that a quiet activity that can help irritability is using art.

Draw it Away

Directions:

Drawing away your feelings is a safe way to let out irritability. Draw a picture of what your irritability feels like or where you feel it inside you. Let out your irritability by pressing the crayon hard onto the paper, using big strokes, or coloring very fast. Choose what the colors that express your irritability the best. When you draw away your anger, it doesn't matter what the picture looks like.

Think of something that you feel very angry about now or that you have been angry about in the past. Draw away your irritability in the space below.

Short Term Goal 2: Help a young person regain interest and pleasure in activities.

Identifying the Losses

Directions:

Counselors working with young children can talk to the child and fill out the chart for them. Counselors working with older children and adolescents should hand the chart and have the young person fill it out. Successful therapy depends in part on the degree of shared involvement in the counseling activities. Young persons need to "own" part of the counseling activities.

Make a list of all the things you used to enjoy doing but now avoid. Rate the degree to which you avoid each item (where 0 = not at all and 10 = completely). Include items that are somewhat uncomfortable (4–7) along with ones you must completely avoid (9–10).

Examples:

Pleasurable Situations or Activities Avoided	Degree Avoided (0–10)
• Playing with my friends	10
• Talking on the phone to friends	6
• Going to movies	7
• Playing on the playground with others	8
• Interacting with others at lunch	8
• Doing my homework or school work	4
• Shopping	10

What I avoid: **Degree Avoided**

_____   _____

_____   _____

_____   _____

_____   _____

_____   _____

_____   _____

_____   _____

_____   _____

Once identified, help the young person discuss the thoughts behind the avoidance:

I used to _____
(description of activity)

I engaged in this activity at least _____
(number of times each week)

I used to enjoy this because _____

_____

_____

Now, I don't do this because _____

_____

_____

What I tell myself about this is _____

_____

_____

My thought is irrational because it contains the following cognitive distortions:

1. _____ All-or-nothing thinking: Looking at things in absolute, black-and-white categories.

2. _____ Overgeneralization: Viewing a negative event as a never-ending pattern of defeat.

3. _____ Mental filter: Dwelling on the negatives and ignoring the positives.

4. _____ Discounting the positives: Insisting that accomplishments or positive qualities "don't count."

5. _____ Jumping to conclusions: (A) Mind reading—assuming that people are reacting negatively to you when there's no evidence for this; (B) Fortune-telling—Arbitrarily predicting that things will turn out badly.

6. _____ Magnification or minimization: Blowing things way up out of proportion or shrinking their importance inappropriately.

7. _____ Emotional reasoning: Reasoning from how you feel: "I feel like an idiot, so I really must be one."

8. _____ "Should Statements": Criticizing yourself or other people with "shoulds" or "shouldn'ts."

9. _____ Labeling: Identifying shortcomings. Instead of saying, "I made a mistake," you tell yourself, "I'm a loser."

10. _____ Personalization and blame: Blaming yourself for something you weren't entirely responsible for, or blaming other people and overlooking ways that your own attitudes and behavior might contribute to the problem.

What I can tell myself instead is _____

_____

_____

What I need to do to change things for myself is:

1. _____

2. _____

3. _____

4. _____

5. _____

My level of commitment to this plan is:

_____   1 Not committed at all

_____   2 Will try this

_____   3 Will do this

_____   4 Want very much to accomplish these things

_____   5 Nothing will stop me

A few things that might keep me from carrying out my plans are: _____

_____

_____

_____

If those things happen, I will: _____

_____

_____

_____

This is my promise for this week.

_____   _____
        (Client signature)   *(Counselor signature)*

Challenging Thoughts That Keep You From Having Fun

Directions:

Once the counselor has worked with a young person in identifying thoughts in situations where the young person has lost interest in pleasurable activities, it is time to start teaching the young person to challenge his or her thoughts and replace them with thoughts that allow them to engage in activities. This is a sheet that should be used in a counseling session and one that should be handed to the young person as a homework exercise.

Example: Challenging your distressing thoughts

Mood Scale 0 = feeling very bad; 10 = feeling very good

Susan's Situation	Susan's thoughts and mood ratings	Susan's improved thoughts and mood ratings
Going to a movie	Why should I go?	If I stay at home, I am doing nothing to help myself.
	The others would prefer I didn't go.	I am jumping to conclusions. My friends keep calling so that is evidence that they want me to go.
	I just don't feel like going.	If I give into my depression I just make myself feel more tired.
	Others think I am no fun.	I am jumping to mind reading here.
	I am too tired.	My emotional reasoning is keeping me from acting.
	My friends never talk to me.	I am overgeneralizing. My friends do talk to me most of the time. When I refuse to see them, they withdraw but this does not happen ALL the time.
	Mood = 2	Mood = 8

By changing Susan's thinking to be more realistic and objective, she was able to feel better about certain situations. This change may not have made Susan entirely happy about going to a movie, but at least it minimized the amount of distress and might allow her the hope she needs to engage once again in a pleasurable activity.

Exercise: Recording and improving your thoughts

Now, you can go over a situation in which you talked yourself out of doing something fun. Note your thoughts, and then try to come up with some new improved thoughts as in the previous examples.

Situation	Thoughts and mood ratings	Improved thoughts and mood ratings
	Mood = _____	Mood = _____

Activity Scheduling

Directions:

Provide this rationale to the young person: Activity scheduling is a way to help you in scheduling various activities into your day-to-day lifestyle. It is often the case that when you are depressed, it is easy to stop doing the things you used to do. Unfortunately, doing less can make you feel more depressed, creating a vicious cycle as the more depressed you feel, the less you feel like doing. We will show you how to break that cycle and get you doing more.

Changing the way you feel by changing the way you behave

The problem with depression is that the symptoms that make up depression also make it difficult for you to start doing something to help yourself. Feeling fatigued, tired and listless makes it difficult to be motivated to help yourself.

Unfortunately it is a vicious cycle—if you feel too tired or listless to do things, you do less and then get upset for doing less. This only makes you feel worse, emotionally and physically, and reduces motivation further.

You must learn how to battle with depressive episodes. If you don't fight the depression, it will overcome you. In this fight you will learn that success comes in small, incremental steps.

Activity is positive, but depression stops you from being active. If you are feeling down, it is sometimes easier to skip going to social activities with others, or to avoid doing the activities you used to enjoy. Unfortunately, this just makes it worse. You need to try and break this vicious cycle.

Activity is positive because it:

- Can make you feel better
- Makes you feel less tired
- Can increase your motivation
- Clears your thinking
- Distracts you from your depressive thoughts

So how do I get myself to do more?

There are a number of things you can do to help you make steps towards recovery. These include activity scheduling, problem solving, and goal setting. (Counselors: these techniques are often used in the CBT framework.)

Activity scheduling

When you become depressed, it is easy to stop doing the things you used to do. Remember that some of the symptoms of depression are fatigue and loss of energy. Thus, it is not surprising that someone with depression lacks the motivation to do things that gives them enjoyment.

The benefits of activity:

- Activity can distract you from depressive thoughts.

- Exercise can make you less tired.

- Activity and exercise can clear the mind and allow more focused thinking.

- Recording what you do now and how much enjoyment you get from the activities you participate in now can assist in identifying the activities that are rated more pleasurable so that they can be scheduled into your daily routine.

Fill it in with the activities you already do. You may find it useful to carry around a small notebook in your pocket to make it easier to remember the various activities that you do.

Rate your enjoyment of the activities using the scale below:

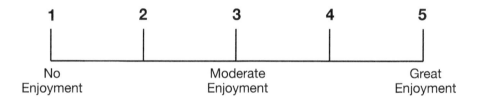

Problem? Can't think of any activity you already do? Ask yourself:

- Are you going to school?

- Do you spend time with friends or family?

- Do you spend time doing homework or school work?

- Do you spend time playing?

- Do you spend time watching TV?

Weekly Timetable

Week beginning _____

Time	Mon.	Tues.	Wed.	Thurs.	Fri.	Sat.	Sun.
8 am							
9 am							
10 am							
11 am							
12 pm							
1 pm							
2 pm							
3 pm							
4 pm							
5 pm							
6 pm							
7 pm							
8 pm							
9 pm							

To do:

- List the activities you usually do.
- Rate your enjoyment on the scale below for the activities you already do.
- If you forgot to fill the diary in, then carry it around in your pocket or bag so you can fill in the activities as you do them.
- Remember you also needed to rate your enjoyment of each activity.
- Keep your completed weekly diary handy as you will need it later on in this session.
- You have already taken the first step by recording what you presently do and how much enjoyment you experienced for each activity. It would be a good idea to find the worksheet where you recorded what you have been doing over the past week. Keep it with you for this session

Scheduling new activities

The idea is to identify what activities you may still enjoy and try to schedule them into your timetable. Are there any activities that you did over the past week that you experienced some enjoyment from? (Look at your completed worksheet from the last session.)

Are there activities you used to enjoy that you no longer participate in? If the answer is yes, then these activities should also be scheduled into your timetable.

It is important to plan your activities in advance—usually a day in advance is sufficient.

WARNING: Do not take on too much too early. Like training for a marathon, you must do it step by step. Master each stage before moving onto the next.

Scheduling pleasant activities

Go through the list in the worksheet below and choose which activities you find pleasant now and those you used to find pleasant but no longer do.

It is important to choose all the activities you once enjoyed doing as well as any that you enjoy now.

Go through the activity list below and mark approximately six activities for you to schedule into your weekly timetable.

Activity List

How to indulge yourself

_____ Do your hair

_____ Paint your nails

_____ Take a bubble bath

_____ Eat your favorite food

_____ Go shopping to buy yourself a little present

_____ Call your friends and plan a date

_____ Buy your favorite book or magazine

_____ Play your favorite computer game

_____ Color in your favorite coloring book

_____ Watch your favorite cartoon or TV show

Energetic activities

_____ Go for a walk

_____ Collect leaves

_____ Play a game

_____ Go for a swim

_____ Go for a bike ride

_____ Go fishing

_____ Take the dog for a walk

_____ Go jogging

_____ Kick a ball around

_____ Plant flowers

_____ Go rollerskating or rollerblading

_____ Lift weights

_____ Play your favorite sport

Activities out and about

_____ Go to a movie

_____ Go shopping

_____ Go out to dinner

_____ Visit the local zoo or theme park

_____ Go to the markets

_____ Go and borrow a book you are interested in from the local library

_____ Go to the art gallery or museum

_____ Watch a sports event you are interested in

_____ Go dancing

Household activities

_____ Do some room cleaning

_____ Do a little gardening

_____ Rearrange the furniture

_____ Organize something that has been bothering you

_____ Do some sewing

_____ Play with your dog or cat

_____ Choose something interesting or novel to cook

Private activities

_____ Listen to music

_____ Dance to some music

_____ Write a letter or email to a friend

_____ Play a computer game

_____ Read a good book, magazine or newspaper

_____ Play a solitary card game

_____ Teach yourself something new

Social activities

_____ Give a friend a call

_____ Meet a friend for coffee or dinner

_____ Go on a picnic with a friend

_____ Play with your friends

_____ Go out with some friends

Add your own examples

_____

_____

_____

_____

_____

_____

Timetabling pleasant activities

Once you have decided which activities you would like to add to your daily schedule, the next step is to plan and schedule them in. Whether you choose to plan your week in advance or just a day in advance, the basic idea is to find a practical way of fitting the enjoyable activities into your daily schedule.

First, write into your schedule all the things that you already do. Once the things you already do have been written into the timetable, it is then time to schedule in the new activities. It is important to choose a time for the new activity(s) when you are most likely to do them.

Record on your timetable:

Example:

Time	Mon.	Tues.	Wed.	Thurs.	Fri.	Sat.	Sun.
1 pm	School	School	School	School	School	Call a friend	TV
2 pm	School	School	School	School	School	Lunch	Lunch & TV
3 pm	Housework	Homework	Homework	Homework	Video games	House-keeping	Read paper
4 pm	Relax	Homework	Homework	Homework	Work	House-keeping	Tidy room
5 pm	*Aerobics Class*	Dinner	Dinner	Dinner	TV	House-keeping	*Go for walk*
6 pm	Go play	Call a friend	Make dinner	Talk to parents	*See a movie*	Dinner	Make dinner
7 pm	Dinner & TV	Dinner & TV	Dinner & TV	Dinner & TV	*See a movie*	Dinner	Make dinner
8 pm	Video game	TV	Video game	TV	Dinner & TV	Rest	TV
9 pm	TV	TV	TV	TV	TV	Rest	TV

When the client returns after the week, as a counselor you would ask to see the timetable and you would ask:

- "Were you able to complete your scheduled activities?"

- "What stopped you?"

- "Let's write down the things or thoughts that stopped you:

   1. _____

   2. _____

   3. _____

   4. _____

   5. _____

- "Let's consider whether you chose the right activity to schedule for you in the first place."

- "Let's brainstorm the ways around the obstacles that stopped you from completing any of the activities one at a time and let's write down ways you can keep these obstacles from stopping you again."

_____

_____

_____

_____

_____

- Now let's create another timetable for the next week.

***Short Term Goal 2:** Help a young person learn to go to sleep and stay asleep and to avoid fatigue brought on by sleep problems.*

Make sure that you understand the differences between insomnia and hypersomnia. Simply stated, insomnia is the inability to fall asleep or stay asleep, the tendency to awaken early in the morning, or the sense of light and non-refreshing sleep. If a teenager stays up all night or a child constantly wakes up at night, then insomnia may be the culprit. Sometimes proper adherence to sleep hygiene rules can be helpful in producing a more rapid resolution to this type of insomnia.

Sleep Hygiene

Examples of sleep hygiene measures include:

- Maintain a regular bedtime schedule.
- Avoid excessive time in bed.
- Avoid taking naps.
- Use the bed only for sleeping.
- Do not watch the clock.
- Do something relaxing before bedtime.
- Make the bedroom as quiet as possible.
- Avoid the consumption of alcohol and caffeine within 12 hours of bedtime
- Exercise moderately, regularly, and not within 4 hours of bedtime.
- Avoid going to bed hungry.
- Learn strategies to make bedtime as relaxing and tension-free as possible.

Progressive Relaxation

Directions:

This exercise is most effective when you tape record the child or adolescent using his or here own voice. In a session tape record the child or adolescent, with a short pause after each sentence (to allow the young person time to actually do the sensing and relaxing). Send the tape home with the young person, instruct the youth to use this right before going to bed each night, and tell him or her:

"Lie on your back, close your eyes, and begin to listen to the tape."

For the recording session, have the young person read these lines into the recorder. Tell the young person that as s/he repeats each statement that s/he should make the body part as tense as possible by clenching all the muscles in that body area, by counting to ten while clenching the muscles, and then relaxing the muscles.

1. I can feel my feet. I can feel the weight of my feet. I can feel my feet relax and sink into the bed.

2. I can feel my lower legs. I can feel the weight of my lower legs. I can feel my lower legs relax and sink into the bed.

3. I can feel my knees. I can feel the weight of my knees. I can feel my knees relax and sink into the bed.

4. I can feel my upper legs. I can feel the weight of my upper legs. I can feel my upper legs relax and sink into the bed.

5. I can feel my hands. I can feel the weight of my hands. I can feel my hands relax and sink into the bed.

6. I can feel my lower arms. I can feel the weight of your lower arms. I can feel my lower arms relax and sink into the bed.

7. I can feel my elbows. I can feel the weight of my elbows. I can feel my elbows relax and sink into the bed.

8. I can feel my upper arms. I can feel the weight of my upper arms. I can feel my upper arms relax and sink into the bed.

9. I can feel my buttocks. I can feel the weight of my buttocks. I can feel my buttocks relax and sink into the bed.

10. I can feel my back. I can feel the weight of my back. I can feel my back relax and sink into the bed.

11. I can feel my belly area. I can feel the weight of my belly area. I can feel my belly area relax and sink into the bed.

12. I can feel my chest. I can feel the weight of my chest. I can feel my chest relax and sink into the bed.

13. I can feel my shoulders. I can feel the weight of my shoulders. I can feel my shoulders relax and sink into the bed.

14. I can feel my neck, both front and back. I can feel the weight of my neck. I can feel my neck relax and sink into the bed.

15. I can feel my skull. I can feel the weight of my skull. I can feel my skull relax and sink into the bed.

16. I can feel my mouth. I can feel any tension in my mouth. I can feel my mouth relax and any tension slide off into the bed.

17. I can feel my eyes. I can feel any tension in my eyes. I can feel my eyes relax and any tension slide off into the bed.

18. I can feel my entire face. I can feel any tension in my face. I can feel my face relax and let any tension slide off into the bed.

Make sure that you remind the client that s/he must tense and relax each body part while listening to the tape.

Progressive Muscle Relaxation for Children (Holistic Psychology)

Directions:

Use the following script to help a child relax.

Today we're going to practice some special kinds of exercises called relaxation exercises. These exercises help you to learn how to relax when you're feeling up-tight and help you get rid of those butterflies-in-your-stomach kinds of feelings. They're also kind of neat because you can learn how to do some of them without anyone really noticing.

In order for you to get the best feelings from these exercises, there are some rules you must follow. First, you must do exactly what I say, even if it seems kind of silly. Second, you must try hard to do what I say. Third, you must pay attention to your body. Throughout these exercises, pay attention to how your muscles feel when they are tight and when they are loose and relaxed. And fourth, you must practice. The more you practice, the more relaxed you can get. Do you have any questions? Are you ready to begin? Okay, first, get as comfortable as you can in your chair. Sit back, get both feet on the floor, and just let your arms hang loose. That's fine. Now close your eyes and don't open them until I say to. Remember to follow my instructions very carefully, try hard, and pay attention to your body. Here we go.

Hands and Arms

Pretend you have a whole lemon in your left hand. Now squeeze it hard. Try to squeeze all the juice out. Feel the tightness in your hand and arm as you squeeze. Now drop the lemon. Notice how your muscles feel when they are relaxed. Take another lemon and squeeze. Try to squeeze this one harder than you did the first one. That's right. Real hard. Now drop the lemon and relax. See how much better your hand and arm feel when they are relaxed. Once again, take a lemon in your left hand and squeeze all the juice out. Don't leave a single drop. Squeeze hard. Good. Now relax and let the lemon fall from your hand.

(Repeat the process for the right hand and arm.)

Arms and Shoulders

Pretend you are a furry, lazy cat. You want to stretch. Stretch your arms out in front of you. Raise them up high over your head. Way back. Feel the pull in your shoulders. Stretch higher. Now just let your arms drop back to your side. Okay, kitten, let's stretch again. Stretch your arms out in front of you. Raise them over your head. Pull them back, way back. Pull hard. Now let them drop quickly. Good. Notice how your shoulders feel more relaxed. This time let's have a great big stretch. Try to touch the ceiling. Stretch your arms way out in front of you. Raise them way up high over your head. Push them way, way back. Notice the tension and pull in your arms and shoulders. Hold tight. Great. Let them drop very quickly and feel how good it is to be relaxed. It feels good, warm and lazy.

Jaw

You have a giant jawbreaker bubble gum in your mouth. It's very hard to chew. Bite down on it. Hard! Let your neck muscles help you. Now relax. Just let your jaw hang loose. Notice that how good it feels just to let your jaw drop. Okay, let's tackle that jawbreaker again. Bite down. Hard! Try to squeeze it out between your teeth. That's good. You're really tearing that gum up. Now relax again. Just let your jaw drop off your face. It feels good just to let go and not have to fight that bubble gum. Okay, one more time. We're really going to tear it up this time. Bite down. Hard as you can. Harder. Oh, you're really working hard. Good. Now relax. Try to relax your whole body. You've beaten that bubble gum. Let yourself go as loose as you can.

Face and Nose

Here comes a pesky old fly. He has landed on your nose. Try to get him off without using your hands. That's right, wrinkle up your nose. Make as many wrinkles in your nose as you can. Scrunch your nose up real hard. Good. You've chased him away. Now you can relax your nose. Oops, here he comes back again. Right back in the middle of your nose. Wrinkle up your nose again. Shoo him off. Wrinkle it up hard. Hold it just as tight as you can. Okay, he flew away. You can relax your face. Notice that when you scrunch up your nose your cheeks and your mouth and your forehead and your eyes all help you, and they get tight too. So when you relax your nose, your whole body relaxes too, and that feels good. Oh-oh. This time that old fly has come back, but this time he's on your forehead. Make lots of wrinkles. Try to catch him between all those wrinkles. Hold it tight, now. Okay, you can let go. He's gone for good. Now you can just relax. Let your face go smooth, no wrinkles anywhere. Your face feels nice and smooth and relaxed.

Stomach

Hey! Here comes a cute baby elephant. But he's not watching where he's going. He doesn't see you lying in the grass, and he's about to step on your stomach. Don't move. You don't have time to get out of the way. Just get ready for him. Make your stomach very hard. Tighten up your stomach muscles real tight. Hold it. It looks like he is going the other way. You can relax now. Let your stomach go soft. Let it be as relaxed as you can. That feels so much better. Oops, he's coming this way again. Get Ready. Tighten up your stomach. Real hard. If he steps on you when your stomach is hard, it won't hurt. Make your stomach hard like a rock. Okay, he's moving away again. You can relax now. Settle down, get comfortable, and relax. Notice the difference between a tight stomach and a relaxed one. That's how we want to feel—nice and loose and relaxed. You won't believe this, but this time he's coming your way and no turning around. He's headed straight for you. Tighten up. Tighten hard. Here he comes. This is really it. You've got to hold on tight. He's stepping on you. He's stepped over you. Now he's gone for good. You can relax completely. You're safe. Everything is okay, and you can feel nice and relaxed.

This time imagine that you want to squeeze through a narrow fence and the boards have splinters on them. You'll have to make yourself very skinny if you're going to make it through. Suck your stomach in. Try to squeeze it up against your backbone. Try to be skinny as you can. You've got to be skinny now. Just relax and feel your stomach being warm and loose. Okay, let's try to get through that fence now. Squeeze up your stomach. Make it touch your backbone. Get it real small and tight. Get it as skinny as you can. Hold tight, now. You've got to squeeze through. You got through that narrow little fence and no splinters! You can relax now. Settle back and let your stomach come back out where it belongs. You can feel really good now. You've done fine.

Legs and Feet

Now pretend that you are standing barefoot in a big, fat mud puddle. Squish your toes down deep into the mud. Try to get your feet down to the bottom of the mud puddle. You'll probably need your legs to help you push. Push down, spread your toes apart, feel the mud squish up between your toes. Now step out of the mud puddle. Relax your feet. Let your toes go loose and feel how nice that it feels to be relaxed. Back into the mud puddle. Squish your toes down. Let your leg muscles help push your feet down. Push your feet. Hard. Try to squeeze that puddle dry. Okay. Come back out now. Relax your feet, relax your legs, relax your toes. It feels so good to be relaxed. No tenseness anywhere. You feel kind of warm and tingly.

Conclusion

Stay as relaxed as you can. Let your whole body go limp and feel all your muscles relaxed. In a few minutes I will ask you to open your eyes, and that will be the end of this practice session. As you go through the day, remember how good it feels to be relaxed. Sometimes you have to make yourself tighter before you can be relaxed, just as we did in these exercises. Practice these exercises everyday to get more and more relaxed. A good time to practice is at night, after you have gone to bed and the lights are out and you won't be disturbed. It will help you get to sleep. Then, when you are really a good relaxer, you can help yourself relax at bedtime. Just remember the elephant, or the jaw breaker, or the mud puddle, and you can do our exercises and nobody will know. Today is a good day, and you are ready to feel very relaxed. You've worked hard and it feels good to work hard. Very slowly, now, open your eyes and wiggle your muscles around a little. Very good. You've done a good job. You're going to be a super relaxer at bedtime.

The Sleep Diary

Directions:

For older children and teenagers, using a sleep diary will help you and the young person get a handle on how the young person handles (or does not handle) sleeping. You would tell the young person that the Sleep Diary is used to take inventory of sleeping patterns. Keep a sleep diary/journal for at least 2 weeks to help identify specific problems. The diary/journal should include: time you go to bed, how long it took to fall asleep, when you wake up, nap times, emotions you felt that day, amount and type of exercise, foods you ate/drank that day (especially note: caffeine, alcohol, nicotine). A sleep diary will help identify patterns in sleep behaviors. The Sleep Diary looks like this:

Answer in the morning after waking for the day

	At what time did you first go to bed?	How long did it take you to fall asleep?	Overall, how many hours did you sleep?	At what time did you wake up (for the last time) this morning?	In general, how did you feel when you woke up? (Very refreshed, somewhat refreshed, fatigued)	On a scale of 1–5, how well did you sleep last night? 5—didn't wake 1—woke four times)
Day 1						
Day 2						
Day 3						
Day 4						
Day 5						
Day 6						
Day 7						

Answer at bedtime just before you go to sleep

	How much time, if any, did you spend napping during the day?	Did you consume any of these substances during the day? • Caffiene (within 6 hours of bedime) • Alcohol (within 1 hour of bedtime) • Type _____ _____	On a scale of 1–5. how would you rate your overall mood and functioning during the day? 5—Positive and energetic 1—Depressed and lethargic)	List all activities within 2 hours of bedtime.
Day 1				
Day 2				
Day 3				
Day 4				
Day 5				
Day 6				
Day 7				

After charting the sleep habits of the youth, discuss anything like naps, caffeine use, etc. that would interfere with sleeping and develop a plan to follow that will help the young person incorporate sleep hygiene habits. The plan would look like this:

I _____ will:

(client's name)

_____ Maintain a regular bedtime schedule.

_____ Avoid excessive time in bed.

_____ Avoid taking naps.

_____ Use the bed only for sleeping.

_____ Will not watch the clock.

_____ Do something relaxing before bedtime. This includes:

_____ Make the bedroom as quiet as possible.

_____ Avoid the consumption of alcohol and caffeine within 12 hours of bedtime

_____ Exercise moderately, regularly, and not within 4 hours of bedtime.

_____ Avoid going to bed hungry.

_____

_____

_____

Hypersomnia is characterized by recurrent episodes of excessive daytime sleepiness or prolonged nighttime sleep. People with hypersomnia are usually compelled to nap repeatedly during the day often at inappropriate times (school, conversation, meals). Hypersomnia usually affects adolescents and young adults. Treatment for hypersomnia includes: changes in behavior, diet, good sleep hygiene and sometimes medication such as: amphetamine, methylphenidate, modafinil, clonidine, levodopa, antidepressants all which require the intervention of a medical doctor.

Short Term Goal 3: Teach youths to overcome feelings of guilt and worthlessness.

Directions:

Talk with the young person and clearly explain to then that throughout life, people will develop an identity and will then attach a value to this identity. A problem arises for some people when they attach a negative value to their identity. They tell themselves that they are worthless, that they can't do anything, that everything is their fault, that they are bad, stupid, or dumb, and all sorts of things that lead to negative feelings and depression.

Tell the young person that judging oneself in a negative way leads to psychological distress or pain. Being in pain may lead to withdrawal from activities that may in turn, exacerbate the pain. Explain that some people protect themselves from situations or people that further increase distress. Examples of mechanisms that people use to protect themselves can include:

- Blaming others for things that go wrong (rather than sharing the blame in some circumstances).
- Getting angry with others.
- Being perfectionistic about work and immersing self in work.
- Bragging to others.
- Making excuses for mistakes.
- Turning to drugs or alcohol to dull the pain.

You need to teach young people that they can change their feelings. The following three exercises are for young children.

Feeling Game

Directions:

Tell the child: Let's play a pretend game about feelings. You will take a turn pretending something happens to you. Then you show how you feel about it using your voice and your body. Watch me pretend a feeling and then guess what I am feeling.

Counselor models: spilling a pretend soda; saying, "Bummer!" and showing a feeling of disgust; and saying, "How do you think I feel?"

Role plays: (Guide the client in acting out the role plays and showing how they would feel in the situation. If there are two roles have the child play the feeling role and you play the other role. If you are in a group, ask the group to guess the feeling.)

- A car honks at you. (afraid)
- You are given a surprise gift. (surprised)
- You accidentally spill soup in the cafeteria. (disgusted)
- Someone jumps out at you. (surprised or afraid)
- You can't find anyone to watch TV with. (sad)
- You open the bag and find mold on bread. (disgusted)
- A friend tells you s/he likes you. (happy)
- You just started a new class and don't know anyone. (afraid, shy)

Do you notice that there are all kinds of feelings? I might have different kinds of feelings than you. For example, when a car honks, I might feel irritated at the person honking the horn or sorry for the driver who is upsetting himself. This has a lot to do with what I tell myself about the situation. For example,

- A car honks at me. Instead of being afraid, I might tell myself:

  "What is wrong with the driver of that car! He is stupid!" and the feeling I would have is a feeling of being irritated.

  Or I might tell myself:

  "The poor guy behind me is making himself all upset over nothing." and the feeling I would have would be feeling sorry for the driver.

- I am given a surprise gift. Instead of being surprised, I might tell myself:

  "Oh no! It must be our anniversary and I forgot to get my husband a card!" and my feeling would be one of dismay.

  Or I might tell myself:

  "It's my birthday and I like it that someone remembered." and my feeling would be one of happiness.

- You accidentally spill soup in the cafeteria what do you tell yourself if you are disgusted?

  _____

  _____

  What could you tell yourself instead and what other feeling would you have?

  _____

  _____

  Sometimes you tell yourself that you are bad or worthless. Write down when that happened last.

  _____

  _____

  Now, write down something else you could tell yourself in that situation.

  _____

  _____

  Do you understand that you can make yourself feel bad and that you can change that feeling? Tell me about other situations where you make yourself feel bad and tell yourself that you are worthless, bad or stupid.

  1. _____

  2. _____

  3. _____

  Tell me what you can say to yourself to change this feeling:

  1. _____

  2. _____

Understanding Similar and Different Feelings

Directions:

Tell the child: Let's play another game. We are going to stand face to face. We are going to pretend something happens to us and we will make a face to show how we feel.

Counselor and then client: Reacting to being served carrots at dinner.

Role play: Have the client go first and then as the counselor model a different feeling.

- A friend wants to show you her huge dog.
- You just found out your parents are going to have another baby.
- A friend rolled down a hill and wants you to join him.
- It's your turn to give a speech in class.
- You are given a big bowl of ice cream.
- You are given a new toy.
- Your uncle just bought your sister a new doll.
- It is your turn to jump in a mud puddle.
- You are given spinach at lunch.
- You are chosen to lead a game.

In each situation each of us had a different feeling. Why do you suppose this is true? (Correct answer: because we tell ourselves different things about each event.)

Sometimes when you feel down, you have to stop telling yourself something that is not helpful.

When was the last time you felt down? What did you tell yourself? Instead of telling yourself that, what could you say to yourself instead? Let's write this down:

_____

_____

_____

_____

_____

Understanding Feelings Change

Directions:

The counselor will suggest a new game. In this game, I will describe a situation and you will tell me how you feel about it and how your feelings might have changed.

Counselor models: changing feelings by saying, "Snakes: I used to feel scared by snakes, now I feel interested in them."

Role plays: Have the client fill in this sentence form:

- "I used to feel _____ about [situation], now I feel _____ about [situation].")
- Climbing high
- Going to bed
- Riding a roller coaster
- Playing with guns
- Meeting a new teacher
- Eating a new food
- Going to the dentist
- Having a babysitter
- Christmas morning
- A whining sister
- Moving to a new town
- Getting a shot
- Swinging on the monkey bars

Now, the last time you told yourself you were stupid, you could say,

"I used to feel stupid about [situation], now I feel _____ about [situation]."

The last time you told yourself you were worthless, you could say,

"I used to feel worthless about [situation], now I feel _____ about [situation]."

The last time you told yourself you were dumb, you could say,

"I used to feel dumb about [situation], now I feel _____ about [situation]."

The last time you told yourself that you were a baby, you could say,

"I used to feel like a baby about [situation], now I feel _____ about [situation]."

Are there any other things you call yourself?

In order to build self-esteem, it is essential for people to stop making judgments about themselves and to let pain disappear and wounds heal. No one gets everything they want in life. Sometimes other people don't do as we wish. Sometimes other people hurt us. That does not mean that we are dumb, stupid, or undeserving. If we feel worthless or guilty we build low self-esteem. Healthy self-esteem is when we accept ourselves for who we are instead of judging ourselves. It is not achieved by compliments from other people, but rather from within. Low self-esteem is wishing you were someone other than yourself.

Factors affecting self-esteem include:

- Thinking in all-or-nothing terms (many other thinking errors apply here)
- Perfectionistic standards
- Inability to be assertive
- Lack of goals and feeling of not getting anywhere

Building self-esteem is directed by targeting the factors that affect self-esteem. You can build self esteem by:

- Stopping yourself from thinking in all-or-nothing terms
- Looking at the perfectionistic standards you set for yourself and making them more realistic
- Building assertiveness skills
- Setting goals for yourself

Thinking in All-or-Nothing Terms Affects Self Esteem

Thinking in all-or-nothing terms: This is black and white thinking, in which everything is either good or bad, right or wrong, and there is no middle ground. The world is not black or white - it is full of shades of gray. Trying to fit the world into black and white terms leaves you feeling very dissatisfied. You are better off to work in shades of gray and avoid using the absolute terms.

Example: I made a 76 on a science test. I am a failure.

- Thinking this way shows that you have very high expectations.

- However, on a grade scale scores range from 0 to 100 points. Making a 76 indicates that you did not fail (black thinking) but that you made an average grade. Maybe you would like to have made a higher grade but you did not fail.

- Keep challenging your thoughts and attempting to make them more rational.

My thought is irrational because it contains the following cognitive distortions:

_____ **All-or-nothing thinking:** Looking at things in absolute, black-and-white categories.

_____ **Personalization and blame:** Blaming yourself for something you weren't entirely responsible for, or blaming other people and overlooking ways that your own attitudes and behavior might contribute to the problem.

What I can tell myself instead is _____

_____

_____

What I need to do to change things for myself is:

1. _____

2. _____

3. _____

4. _____

5. _____

My level of commitment to this plan is:

_____ 1 Not committed at all

_____ 2 Will try this

_____ 3 Will do this

_____ 4 Want very much to accomplish these things

_____ 5 Nothing will stop me

A few things that might keep me from carrying out my plans are: _____

_____

_____

_____

If those things happen, I will: _____

_____

_____

_____

This is my promise for this week.

_____   _____
(Client signature)   *(Counselor signature)*

Perfectionistic Standards and What You Can Do

- A perfectionist is someone who places a lot of emphasis on completing tasks just right. Perfectionistic standards place a lot of pressure on the individual, as the standard is very difficult to live up to.

- Perfectionism can impede getting the work done. This is because it can take much longer to finish a task when your standards are exceptionally high.

- Do you set perfectionistic standards for others? If you do, you will probably find that others rarely live up to your expectations for them.

- Often, a perfectionistic drive is driven by fears such as:
  - Fear of disappointing others
  - Fear of losing control
  - Fear of not getting approval from others

What can you do to fight the perfectionistic urge?

1. Attempt a task and deliberately expect less from yourself. Finish the assignment without proofreading it a second time, or submit work to your teacher that you've spent a lot of time on, but still feel like going over again.

2. Think about what might be driving your fears and need for perfectionism. Can you see any patterns?

3. Set time limits for tasks. For example, I will clean my room for one hour only.

4. Deliberately leave something not quite right and try to cope with your resulting distress. Try to get used to finishing tasks at a lower level.

5. Admit to someone else that you are not perfect! How do they react?

6. Take time to smell the flowers! Enjoy the task you are doing rather than focusing on completing it.

Setting Goals

Directions:

Tell the client the following facts:

- We all need goals to work toward.

- We have no way of evaluating if we are getting somewhere unless we can see if we have made it to our goals.

- It is important to set small goals. If the goals are too overwhelming, it will do more harm than good.

- Goals only assist us if they are flexible and re-evaluated as time passes. If the goals are rigid, then they can do more harm than good.

Area	Short term (Next week)	Mid term (Next month)	Long term (Next year)
Recreational Activities			
Family Life			
Health			
Relationships			
Personal Development			
School			

Once you have set some goals for yourself, it is easier to try and work out what the intervening steps would be to achieve them.

Remember, as time goes on, you may need to stop and re-evaluate your goals.

Self-esteem Raisers

Directions:

Fill in the blanks below. Try to recognize your strengths. It is not an easy task to identify positive characteristics in yourself, as it is not rewarded in today's society. However, it is important you persist and not give up.

Liking yourself is the essence of self-esteem

1. I do _____ well.

2. I feel good about _____.

3. What I enjoy most is _____.

4. One of the positive characteristics I have is _____.

5. What I do best is _____.

6. My friends respect me because _____.

7. I will be successful because _____.

8. Others have told me that I have attractive _____.

9. Others say that I am good at _____.

10. Others often compliment me about _____.

11. The one person that makes me feel good about myself the most is _____.

12. I admire _____ the most.

13. I feel good about myself when _____.

14. My favorite place is _____.

15. My goals for the future are _____.

16. I look good when I _____.

17. _____ likes me.

18. _____ loves me.

19. My strength is _____.

20. I excel at _____.

Exercise: Identifying Thoughts That Make You Feel Worthless or Guilty

Directions:

Think of a time when you felt bad or distressed. What was going on at the time? Write this situation or event in the situation column. Ask yourself the following questions:

1. What do you think about yourself?

2. Is there anyone else involved in the situation? If so, what do you think about them?

3. What do you think that others think of you?

4. What do you think about the situation?

   - How did you feel? Write this in the Feeling column.

   - Now think hard about what thoughts you had at the time. Write these thoughts in the middle column.

   - Try doing this for two separate occasions when you felt distressed or upset.

Situation	Thoughts	Feelings

Would others react the same way that you did?

Ask yourself:

- How do you think someone else would feel if they had the same thought as you?

- How would someone else feel if you told him/her the thought you had?

Most likely, you will be able to see that not everyone would think or feel the same after experiencing the same situation or event.

Once you have had a little practice identifying your thoughts in situations when you feel distressed, it is time to start challenging your thoughts and replacing them with thoughts that are less distressing.

Affirmation Collage

Directions:

An affirmation collage is a tool we use to visualize how we see ourselves and the manner in which we experience our lives. You will develop an affirmation collage that will be a picture of how you see yourself right now. It can contain pictures, words, or symbols that are a reflection of those qualities that express you. Then we will make a second collage showing how you wish you were, showing the qualities you want to attain, and the goals you want to achieve in your life. We will cut out pictures and word symbols from magazines, catalogs, newspapers, and old books and glue them together so that you can show me how you see your life right now and how you would like to see your life.

Select one page to represent each aspect of your life as you see yourself right now and another page to represent yourself the way you would like to be. Choose appropriate pictures to express the particular feeling, quality, goal, or material item you want to share. Let your imagination soar. Glue the pictures to the pages.

Now, let's look at the pictures and you explain the differences in yourself now and how you would like to be in the future. We will use this chart:

The Way I Am	The Way I Would Like to Be

One at a time, let's take the way you are and have you tell me what steps you could take to become the way you would like to be:

1. I am _____

   _____

   In order to change I must::

       1. _____

       2. _____

       3. _____

2. I am _____

   _____

   In order to change I must::

       1. _____

       2. _____

       3. _____

3. I am _____

   _____

   In order to change I must::

       1. _____

       2. _____

       3. _____

4. I am _____

   _____

   In order to change I must::

       1. _____

       2. _____

       3. _____

5. I am _____

_____

In order to change I must::

    1. _____

    2. _____

    3. _____

6. I am _____

_____

In order to change I must::

    1. _____

    2. _____

    3. _____

7. I am _____

_____

In order to change I must::

    1. _____

    2. _____

    3. _____

8. I am _____

_____

In order to change I must::

    1. _____

    2. _____

    3. _____

9. I am _____

_____

In order to change I must::

    1. _____

    2. _____

    3. _____

10. I am _____

_____

In order to change I must::

    1. _____

    2. _____

    3. _____

Now out of these ten things you want to change, choose the one you will work on and sign this page showing me that you intend to change this one thing this next week.

I, _____, will work on change item number _____.

          (Client signature)   *(Item #)*

Song Affirmation

Directions:

This is just like the Affirmation Collage, but instead of giving the client paper and magazines to allow them self-expression, you hand them a tape recorder and tell them to record songs that will show you who they are right now. When they have the selection of songs, they will fill out the following form and bring both the form and the music back to you. In a session, you have them play the song and talk to you about their comments about themselves.

Title of Song _____

What it says about me: _____

_____

_____

Title of Song _____

What it says about me: _____

_____

_____

Title of Song _____

What it says about me: _____

_____

_____

Then have the client choose and record songs explaining how they would like to be.

When they have the selection of songs, they will fill out the following form and bring both the form and the music back to you. In a session, you have them play the song and talk to you about their comments about themselves.

Title of Song _____

What it tells you about the way I would like to be: _____

_____

_____

Title of Song _____

What it tells you about the way I would like to be: _____

_____

_____

Title of Song _____

What it tells you about the way I would like to be: _____

_____

_____

One at a time, let's take the way you are and have you tell me what steps you could take to become the way you would like to be:

1. I am _____

_____

In order to change I must::

    1. _____

    2. _____

    3. _____

2. I am _____

_____

In order to change I must::

    1. _____

    2. _____

    3. _____

3. I am _____

_____

In order to change I must::

   1. _____

   2. _____

   3. _____

4. I am _____

_____

In order to change I must::

   1. _____

   2. _____

   3. _____

5. I am _____

_____

In order to change I must::

   1. _____

   2. _____

   3. _____

Now out of these five things you want to change, choose the one you will work on and sign this page showing me that you intend to change this one thing this next week.

I, _____, will work on change item number _____.

(Client signature)   *(Item #)*

Short Term Goal 4: Teach youths to concentrate and make decisions

Help with Poor Concentration

Directions:

Worry or Think Time Strategy

Set aside a specific time each day to think about the things that keep entering your mind and interfering with your concentration. For example, set 4:30 to 5:00 p.m. as your worry/think-time. When your mind is side-tracked into worrying during the day, remind yourself that you have a special time for worrying. Then, let the thought go for the present, and return your concentration and focus to your immediate activity.

The important steps are:

1. Set a specific time each day for your time.

2. When you become aware of a distracting thought, remind yourself that you have a special time to think about them. Have a paper pad and pen handy to jot them down so you'll be sure to remember them.

3. Let the thought go, perhaps with "Stop Thinking"(strategy described on the following page).

4. Be sure to keep that appointment with yourself at that special time to think on the distracting thoughts of the day.

"Stop Thinking" Strategy

This deceptively simple strategy is probably the most effective. When you notice your thoughts wandering astray, say to yourself . . .

"Stop Thinking This"

. . . and gently bring your attention back to where you want it.

For example:

You're in class and your concentration and attention strays from the lecture to all the homework you have, to a date, to the fact that you're hungry. As you say to yourself . . .

"Stop Thinking This"

. . . you focus back on the lecture and maintain your concentration there as long as possible.

When it wanders again, repeat . . .

"Stop Thinking This"

. . . and gently bring your concentration back.

You may notice that your mind often wanders (as often as several times a minute at times). Each time just say . . .

"Stop Thinking This"

. . . and refocus. Do not try to keep particular thoughts out of your mind. For example, as you sit there, close your eyes and think about anything you want to for the next three minutes except cookies. Try not to think about cookies. When you try not to think about something, it keeps coming back. *("I'm not going to think about cookies. I'm not going to think about cookies.")*

When you find your thoughts wandering, gently let go of that thought and, with your . . .

"Stop Thinking This"

. . . return to the present.

You might do this hundreds of times a week, if you're normal. But, you'll find that the period of time between your straying thoughts gets a little longer every few days. So be patient and keep at it. You'll see some improvement in your concentration!

Shape Holding Strategy

This is an exercise to improve your ability to focus and concentrate on body feel and position, relative to the outside world.

For this exercise you will need:

- A blank piece of paper (bigger than your hand).

- A pencil

Steps:

1. Touch the paper will all your fingertips and thumb of your non-writing hand. Move them around a bit until the shape is distinctly awkward.

2. With the pencil, draw around each finger sufficiently to be able to see where the fingers were.

3. Holding your non-writing fingers in the same shape, take them off the paper, and hold up the hand.

4. Close your eyes and hold that shape for 15 seconds.

5. Without opening your eyes, put your fingers back on the paper.

6. Open your eyes and check how you did.

Variations of this exercise can include anything from toes to your whole body, if you can find a way of checking the position.

Five Finger Exercise

(Western Washington University, 2003)

Sit back, take a few deep breaths and then establish an easy, regular breathing pattern.

To begin, take a deep breath and as you exhale, touch your thumb to your index finger. Recall a time when your body felt a healthy fatigue, like how you felt after exercising, or just stepping out of a sauna or hot tub.

Next, take another deep breath, and as you exhale, touch your thumb to your middle finger and go back to a time when you had a loving experience, a time when you felt a strong sense of closeness or connection. This could be a spiritual experience while you were alone or feelings of love toward another person. Take a moment to feel that feeling as vividly as you can.

Now take another deep breath, and as you exhale, touch your thumb to your ring finger and recall a time when you performed very well, when you mastered something and received recognition for your work. Take that sense of accomplishment in now, feel it fully and know that you deserved it.

Finally, take one more deep breath in and as you exhale, touch your thumb to your little finger and as you do, recall the most beautiful place you have ever been...or imagine how such a place would look and feel if you were there now. Take a moment to absorb the full feeling of this place, and when you're ready, bringing with you the feelings you would like to feel for the rest of your day, come back.

This peaceful and tranquil state should help you to relax and give your concentration and focus to the task you perform following this exercise.

Focus on Your Breath Exercise

Directions:

Tell your client that this is a basic concentration practice. It's also the first step of relaxation exercises. It's good to use at the beginning of a study session to put yourself in a good frame of mind. By practicing this, you can develop a very practical skill of mind and body for unstressing yourself. Practice the quick procedure whenever you feel yourself becoming tense. The procedure involves taking 5 long, slow breaths while noticing tension and relaxing your body.

Before you begin:

Slowly stretch out your arms and legs, fingers and toes. Now take a slow, leisurely yawn.

Steps:

Breath #1. Take in a long, slow breath while counting to six. Breathe deeply into your stomach and hold your breath for a few seconds. Now let the air flow out slowly as you give yourself permission to "relax".

Breath #2. As you take in another long, slow breath, concentrate on the muscles in your scalp, forehead, eyes, mouth and face. Notice any tension you may be holding...and relax these areas as you exhale slowly, giving yourself permission to let go and "relax".

Breath #3. As you take in a long, slow breath, concentrate on the muscles in your neck and shoulders. Now release the tension in these muscles as you exhale slowly, as you give yourself permission to "relax."

Breath #4. As you take in a long, slow breath, concentrate on any tension in the muscles in your chest and abdomen. Relax these muscles as you exhale, again giving yourself permission to let go and "relax".

Breath #5. As you take in another long, slow breath, notice muscular tension anywhere in your body. Hold the breath for a few seconds, and then exhale slowly while giving yourself permission to "relax."

Now that you have relaxed, tell yourself to focus and begin to pay attention to the matter at hand, whether it is completing an assignment, writing down notes, listening to another person, or working out a problem on a test.

Every time you feel your attention slipping away, go back to the exercise and repeat it once again.

"Brain Buttons" Exercise

Directions:

Explain this to your client: Our bodies are very much a part of all our learning, and learning is not an isolated "brain" function. Every nerve and cell is a network contributing to our intelligence and our learning capability. Many educators have found this exercise quite helpful in improving overall concentration in class. This exercise can be used quickly in any classroom. It is surprisingly simple, but very effective!

More specifically, this exercise helps improve blood flow to the brain to "switch on" the entire brain before a lesson begins. The increased blood flow helps improve concentration skills required for reading, writing, and etc.

Steps:

1. Take one hand and stretch out your digits as far as you can so that there is as wide of a space as possible between the thumb and index finger.

2. With your other hand, place your thumb and first finger over the space between your thumb and finger and squeeze hard.

3. Squeeze hard and count slowly to ten.

4. Then shake your hand.

5. Whenever you find your mind wandering, repeat this exercise.

Pros and Cons Decision-Making Method

Directions:

Explain: A simple process for decision-making is the pros and cons list.

Some decisions are a simple matter of whether to make a change or not, such as moving, taking a new job, or buying something, selling something, replacing something, etc. Other decisions involve a number of options, and are concerned more with how to do something, involving a number of choices.

Steps:

1. First you will need a separate sheet of paper for each identified option.

2. On each sheet write clearly the option concerned, and then beneath it the headings 'pros' and 'cons' (or 'advantages' and 'disadvantages', or simply 'for' and 'against'). Many decisions simply involve the choice of whether to go ahead or not, to change or not; in these cases you need only one sheet.

3. Then write down as many effects and implications of the particular option that you (and others if appropriate) can think of, placing each in the relevant column.

4. If helpful, 'weight' each factor by giving it a score out of three or five points (eg., 5 being extremely significant, and 1 being of minor significance).

5. When you have listed all the points you can think of for the option concerned compare the number or total score of the items/effects/factors between the two columns.

6. This will provide a reflection and indication as to the overall attractiveness and benefit of the option concerned. If you have scored each item you will actually be able to arrive at a total score, being the difference between the pros and cons column totals. The bigger the difference between the total pros and total cons then the more attractive the option is.

7. If you have a number of options and have complete a pros and cons sheet for each option, compare the attractiveness—points difference between pros and cons—for each option. The biggest positive difference between pros and cons is the most attractive option.

8. If you don't like the answer that the decision-making sheet(s) reflect back to you, it means you haven't included all the cons—especially the emotional ones, or you haven't scored the factors consistently, so re-visit the sheet(s) concerned.

You will find that writing things down in this way will help you to see things more clearly, become more objective and detached, which will help you to make clearer decisions.

Below is an example of a pros and cons weighted decision-making sheet

Decision Option: Should I Take Senior English	
Pros	**Cons**
Help me get into college. (5)	Too much homework. (5)
Have my favorite teacher. (3)	Want to work. (3)
Lots of my friends are in the class. (4)	Time and hassle. (2)
Write better papers. (3)	Big decisions scare me. (4)
Sit next to Judy. (3)	Big decisions like this scare and upset me.
It'll be a load off my mind. (2)	
Total 6 pros, total score 20	**Total 4 cons, total score 14**

On the basis of the pros and cons, and the weighting applied, in the above example there's a clear overall quantifiable benefit attached to the decision to go ahead and take Senior English. Notice that it's even possible to include 'intangible' emotional issues in the pros and cons comparison, for example 'it'll be a load off my mind,' and 'decisions scare and upset me'. A decision-making pros and cons list like this helps remove the emotion which blocks clear thinking and decision-making.

Decision Tree Analysis

(Mind Tools, 2004)

Choosing Between Options by Projecting Likely Outcomes

Decision Trees are excellent tools for helping you to choose between several courses of action. They provide a highly effective structure within which you can lay out options and investigate the possible outcomes of choosing those options. They also help you to form a balanced picture of the risks and rewards associated with each possible course of action.

How to draw a Decision Tree:

Steps:

1. Begin with a decision that you need to make.

2. Draw a small square to represent this toward the left of a large piece of paper.

3. From this box draw out lines towards the right for each possible solution, and write that solution along the line. Keep the lines as far apart as possible so that you can expand your thoughts.

4. At the end of each line, consider the results. If the result is another decision that you need to make, draw another square. Squares represent decisions.

5. Write the decision or factor above the square or circle. If you have completed the solution at the end of the line, just leave it blank.

6. Starting from the new decision squares on your diagram, draw out lines representing the options that you could select. Again make a brief note on the line saying what it means.

Keep on doing this until you have drawn out as many of the possible decisions as you can see leading off from the original decisions.

An example is shown below:

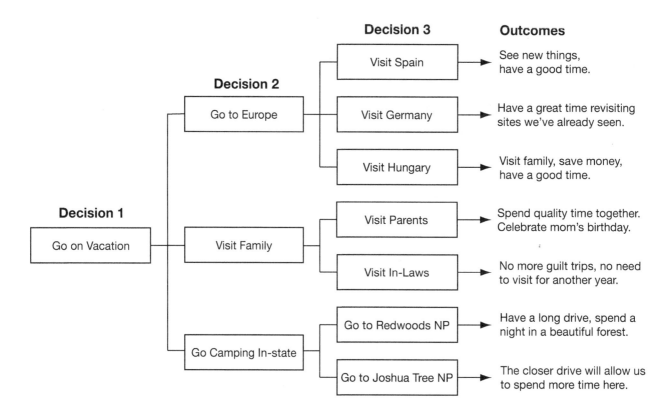

Once you have done this, review your tree diagram. Challenge each square to see if there are any solutions or outcomes you have not considered. If there are, draw them in. If necessary, redraft your tree if parts of it are too congested or untidy. You should now have a good understanding of the range of possible outcomes of your decisions.

Evaluating Your Decision Tree

Now you are ready to evaluate the decision tree. This is where you can work out which option has the greatest worth to you. Start by assigning a cash value or score to each possible outcome. Estimate how much you think it would be worth to you if that outcome came about.

Calculating Tree Values

Once you have worked out the value of the outcomes it is time to start calculating the values that will help you make your decision.

Start on the right hand side of the decision tree, and work back towards the left. As you complete a set of calculations on a node (decision square), all you need to do is to record the result. You can ignore all the calculations that lead to that result from then on.

Key points:

Decision trees provide an effective method of Decision-Making because they:

- Clearly lay out the problem so that all options can be challenged

- Provide a framework to quantify the values of outcomes

- Help us to make the best decisions on the basis of existing information and best guesses.

As with all Decision-Making methods, decision tree analysis should be used in conjunction with common sense.

Cause & Effect Worksheet
Identifying Causes of Problems

Directions:

This Cause & Effect Worksheet helps you to think through causes of a problem thoroughly. Their major benefit is that they push you to consider all possible causes of the problem, rather than just the ones that are most obvious.

Follow these steps to solve a problem:

1. Identify the problem:

   Write down the exact problem you face in detail. Where appropriate identify who is involved, what the problem is, and when and where it occurs.

   Those involved are: _____

   _____

   _____

   The exact problem is: _____

   _____

   _____

   It happens when _____

   _____ at _____

   _____

2. Work out the major factors involved:

   Next identify the factors that may contribute to the problem. Try to draw out as many possible factors as possible.

   The things that contribute to the problem are: _____

   _____

   _____

   _____

3. Identify possible causes:

For each of the factors you considered in stage 2, brainstorm possible causes of the problem that may be related to the factor.

Causes of the problem are: _____

_____

_____

_____

4. Analyze your diagram:

Possible solutions to the problem include: _____

_____

_____

_____

Short Term Goal 5: Help a child or an adolescent deal with thoughts of death and suicidal ideation.

According to Jacobs, Brewer, & Klein-Benheim (1998) effective clinical intervention into potential suicide requires specific information that can help in estimating the intensity of suicidal ideation and intent. Many physicians and even mental health professionals are reluctant to inquire about suicide, perhaps for fear of provoking risk not otherwise present but, more likely, out of discomfort. Suicidal ideas are not new to suicidal persons, and many potential victims will share some of their suicidal thoughts, even if reluctantly. Evaluation should follow a hierarchical assessment, based on simple direct questions concerning thoughts about life at the moment, current level of life dissatisfaction, presence of thoughts about death, preoccupation with self-harm or escape, and the formulation of specific plans and access to a method of self-destruction.

If answers to the preceding inquiries suggest that suicide is likely, the patient must be reassured that help is available and that the clinician is interested in knowing more about his or her despair, takes these suicidal feelings seriously, and will remain available to assist in working out possible interventions. Well-intentioned comments pertaining to hurtful consequences of suicide to others should be avoided because they can increase already excessive guilt and desperation. Superficial minimizing of the potential seriousness of suicidal feelings intended as reassurance is also dangerous. It is also wise to withhold judgment about lethality and intent, since these factors are not readily assessed, can change quickly, and may not reliably predict future behavior. Persons in despair and contemplating suicide need help, and usually gain comfort by being listened to and taken seriously.

Effective assessment for suicide risk also includes attempts to assess levels of intent and lethality, based on evaluating the nature of and access to a proposed method, and the presence of other persons, particularly family members or friends who may be able to prevent a suicidal act or offer additional support. The presence of a detailed suicidal plan, preparation of notes, or clearing up personal or business matters pertaining to survivors are especially ominous occurrences. Interventions are guided by the mental competence and cooperation of the potentially suicidal person, based on clinical assessment of his judgment, comprehension of the circumstances and recommendations; and the likelihood of cooperation and adherence to recommendations. Clinicians who do not feel they are competent to manage a suicidal person can seek consultation or referral to a mental health specialist or make use of specialized healthcare institutions.

Psychological theories about suicide have directed psychodynamic and cognitive-behavioral psychotherapeutic interventions to minimize suicidal risk in at-risk persons. Usually, these efforts aim to decrease anxiety associated with thoughts of death, mobilize defenses against them, and improve problem-solving and coping strategies. An essential implied element of such interventions is support through availability and consistency of the therapist. Isolation should be avoided, daily activities maintained, and the patient reminded repeatedly when depression is the basis of the suicidal ideation that it can be treated. Such therapeutic work typically provokes a conflict between the patient who wants to die and the therapist who seeks to protect life, with intense countertransference responses. According to Hendin, Lipschitz, Maltsberger, Haas, & Wynecoop (2000) dealing directly with thoughts of death may be disturbing for a therapist and provoke his or her own fears of death or failure, feelings of helpless despair, retaliatory anger, or impulses to collaborate with a suicide, thus safe intervention. With that said, whenever you encounter a teenager or child with suicidal ideation, know the warning signs, stay with the youth until you are sure there is no danger, notify caregivers, have a complete assessment done by a competent professional, and decide if you can offer supportive therapy.

The Warning Signs and Risk Factors of Suicide

Demographic or social factors

- Young and elderly men
- Native American or Caucasian
- Being single (widowed > divorced > separated > single)
- Social isolation, including new or worsening estrangement, and rural location
- Economic or occupational stress, losses, or humiliation
- New incarceration
- History of gambling
- Easy access to a firearm

Clinical factors

- Past and current major psychiatric illness (especially depressive)
- Personality disorder (borderline, narcissistic, antisocial)
- Impulsive or violent traits by history
- Current medical illness
- Family history of suicide
- Previous suicide attempts or other self-injurious or impulsive acts
- Current anger, agitation, or constricted preoccupation
- Current abuse of alcohol or drugs or heavy smoking
- Easy access to lethal toxins (including prescribed medicines)
- Formulated plan, preparations for death, or suicide note
- Low ambivalence about dying vs living

Factors specific to youth

- All of the above, less racial difference
- Recent marriage, unwanted pregnancy
- Lack of family support
- History of abuse
- School problems
- Social ostracism, humiliation
- Conduct disorder
- Homosexual orientation

Precipitants

- Recent stressors (especially losses of emotional, social, physical, or financial security)

Protective Factors

- Intact social supports, marriage
- Active religious affiliation or faith
- Presence of dependent young children
- Ongoing supportive relationship with a caregiver
- Absence of depression or substance abuse
- Living close to medical and mental health resources
- Awareness that suicide is a product of illness
- Proven problem-solving and coping skills

Unfortunately, *suicide* has become much more common in children than it used to be. For children under age 15, in the U.S. about 1–2 out of every 100,000 children will *commit* suicide. For those 15–19, about 11 out of 100,000 will commit suicide. Suicide is the fourth leading cause of death for children ages 10–14 and the third leading cause of death for teenagers 15–19. Recent evidence suggests it is the lack of substance abuse, guns, and relationship problems in younger children which accounts for the lower suicide rates in this group.

Lethality

The main way *children kill themselves* depends on what lethal means are available and their age. In countries where guns are readily available, such as the USA, that is the usual cause of suicide. Other causes are strangling and poisoning. The youngest reported intentional suicide has been a six-year-old who hung himself.

Suicide Attempts

Suicide attempts that do not result in death are more common. In any one year, 2–6% of children will try to kill themselves. About 1% of children who try to kill themselves actually die of suicide on the first attempt. On the other hand, of those who have tried to kill themselves repeatedly, 4% succeed. About 15–50% of *children who are attempting suicide* have tried it before. That means that for every 300 suicide attempts, there is one completed suicide.

What makes a child more likely to attempt suicide?

If a *child has major depressive disorder*, he or she is seven times more likely to try suicide. About 22% of *depressed children will try suicide*. Looking at it another way, children and *teenagers who attempt suicide* are 8 times more likely to have a mood disorder, three times more likely to have an *anxiety disorder*, and 6 times more likely to have a *substance abuse problem*.

Problems

A *family history of suicidal behavior* and guns that are available also increase the risk. The vast majority (almost 90%) of children and adolescents who attempt suicide have psychiatric disorders. Over 75% have had some psychiatric contact in the last year.

Myth

Many people have thought that the main reason that *children and adolescents try to kill themselves* is to manipulate others or get attention or as a "cry for help". However, when children and adolescents are actually asked right after their suicide attempts, their *reasons for trying suicide are more like adults*. For a third, their main reason for trying to kill themselves is they wanted to die. Another third wanted to escape from a hopeless situation or a horrible state of mind.

Attention Seeking

Only about 10% were trying to get attention. Only 2% saw getting help as the chief reason for trying suicide. The children who truly wanted to die were more depressed, more angry, and were more perfectionistic.

Suicidal Thinking

This means a person is thinking about suicide but has no plan. This is not uncommon. About 3–4% of adolescents will have considered suicide in the last two weeks. However, these thoughts are much more likely, and more likely to be serious, if the child has previously made a suicide attempt is depressed, or is pessimistic. Children who are still depressed and have made previous suicide attempts are extremely likely to be thinking seriously about suicide.

Three Factors Affecting the Thinking of Young People

Adolescent egocentrism, the imaginary audience and the personal fable may be unique to young people who think about suicide.

Adolescent Egocentrism

Adolescents have a tendency to define the world only as it applies to them. They become preoccupied with their own thought process. They view the world only in terms of: How does this affect me? (Elkind,1967).

The Imaginary Audience

Being preoccupied with their own thinking and self-consciousness about physical and sexual changes, teens often create an imaginary audience and believe that they are continually under observation by others. They anticipate the reactions of others as if others see them as they see themselves. They think that others are as intensely interested in the minutiae details of their appearance and behavior as they are (Manaster, 1977).

The Personal Fable

Teens fail to separate their concerns from those of others. They over differentiate their own feelings and see themselves as new and different than anyone else. Therefore, they regard them-selves as special and unique—a one-of-a-kind individual whom no one else can quite understand. This can lead to the feeling that they are immune from the bad things that happen in life or that nothing will ever really happen to them (Elkind, 1970).

Suicidal Ideation

Take any adolescent who is quite depressed. This teenager will have the symptoms discussed throughout this book. She sleeps poorly, she has no energy, can't concentrate on her work and is super cranky. She thinks about running away or how nice it would be to out of this horrible life. She thinks sometimes about killing herself, but she doesn't think about how she might do it. At the moment, she says she is too scared to actually do something. This is suicidal thinking. Teens like this will be involved in their own thinking and lost in their egocentrism.

The Characteristics

It will be important to understand these characteristics and not dismiss them as we might because we have experienced life and we realize that most people are too involved in themselves to be watching others that closely, that bad things do happen and we can learn to cope, that we don't always get what we want in life and often we have to work hard to make life work and that life just isn't about us. While we listen to others we must truly enter their phenomenological world. We can't go to sleep at the wheel.

Working with Suicidal Ideation

Directions:

As a counselor who might have someone walk through your door and mention suicide, you must engage in an assessment of that child or adolescent before you allow them to leave your office. You have to develop your best clinical judgment about their potential for risk. You will assess their plan for suicide.

Plan Assessment

Assess antecedents of previous suicide attempt(s). Ask:

1. When did you begin to have suicidal thoughts?
2. Did any event (stressor) precipitate these suicidal thoughts?

Determine Present State of Mind. Ask:

1. How often do you think about suicide? Do you feel as if you're a burden? Or that life isn't worth living?
2. What makes you feel better (e.g., contact with family, use of substances)?
3. What makes you feel worse (e.g., being alone)?
4. Do you have a plan to end your life?
5. How much control of your suicidal ideas do you have? Can you suppress them or call someone for help?
6. What stops you from killing yourself (e.g., family, religious beliefs)?

Assess Personal Coping. Direct or ask:

1. Tell me about your relationships with friends and family.
2. Do you prefer being alone or being with friends?
3. Do you have a close friend or relative with whom you have shared your thoughts and feelings?
4. How do you behave when you are sad? Angry? Happy?
5. Tell me, how is school going?

The Plan

You must determine how specific a suicidal plan is. Does the child have a plan? When does s/he intend to kill himself/herself? Does the child have the means? The more specific the plan, the more danger there is.

Delineate the Extent of Ideation. Ask:

1. When did you begin to have suicidal thoughts?

2. Did any event (stressor) precipitate the suicidal thoughts?

3. How often do you think about suicide? Do you feel as if you're a burden? Or that life isn't worth living?

4. What makes you feel better (e.g., contact with family, use of substances)?

5. What makes you feel worse (e.g., being alone)?

6. Do you have a plan to end your life?

7. How much control of your suicidal ideas do you have? Can you suppress them or call someone for help?

8. What stops you from killing yourself (e.g., family, religious beliefs)?

9. Do you own a gun or have access to firearms?

10. Do you have access to potentially harmful medications?

11. Have you "practiced" your suicide? (e.g., put the gun to your head or held the medications in your hand)?

Supervision

DO STAY with the client, and if possible, assist with transfer to appropriate mental health professional. The client has placed trust in you, so you must help transfer that trust to another person. If a child makes a suicide attempt or has a plan, you need to make sure they are not alone. They need to be watched until they can be carefully assessed. This may just be a matter of a day or so, or it could be longer. No one likes being watched all the time, and it is exhausting to all concerned.

The Do Nots

- DON'T leave the client alone for even a minute.

- DON'T act shocked, allow yourself to be sworn to secrecy, or brush aside a threat.

- DON'T let the client convince you that the crisis is over. Often the most dangerous time is precisely when the person seems to be feeling better. Sometimes the client may appear happy and relaxed simply because they have come to a decision (even if that decision is suicide).

High Risk

If the teen is holding on to dangerous items, it is the highest risk situation. You should call an ambulance, police and the client's parents. You should try to calm the client and ask for the dangerous items. If the client has no dangerous objects, but appears to be an immediate suicide risk, it would be considered a high-risk situation. If the client is upset because of *physical or sexual abuse,* you must, by most state laws, notify the Child Protective Services. If there is no evidence of abuse or neglect, you should contact parents and ask them to come in to pick up their child.

Talking to Parents

You should inform them fully about the situation and strongly encourage them to take their child to an appropriate mental health professional or facility for an evaluation. You should give the parents a list of telephone numbers of crisis clinics. If you are unable to contact parents, and if Protective Services or the police cannot intervene, designated staff should take the client to a nearby emergency room.

Talk to the Child or Teen

Spending time just talking to the child or teen is important. Questions to ask:

1. "Seems like you've been having a hard time lately, what's going on?" (to establish rapport and trust and to open dialog in a non-threatening way)

2. "What is your understanding of why you have been asked to come to the office?" (to review factual events)

3. "What is your understanding of why school staff are concerned?" (to determine if student is aware of effect behavior has on others)

4. "What has been going on recently with you at school?" (to look into possible precipitating events such as peer conflict, student/teacher interactions, failing grades, etc.; follow appropriate leads)

5. "How are things going with your family?" (to look into events such as recent moves, divorce, deaths or losses, conflict)

6. "What else is going on with you?" (to look into events outside of school such as community unrest, threats, police involvement, medical issues, etc.)

7. "Who do you have to talk to or assist you with this situation?" (to determine what supports or stabilizing factors may be available or in place such as mental health professionals, peer groups, family supports, church groups, etc.)

8. "Given (whatever is going on), what are you planning to do?" or, "What are you thinking about doing?" (follow-up on appropriate leads, including the level of detail in stated plans, ability to carry out plans, etc.) (NOTE: If there is an IMMINENT RISK take immediate action to maintain safety by contacting security and/or 911).

Provide Self-Help Tips About Feeling Suicidal:

1. Tell your therapist, a friend, a family member, or someone else who can help.

2. Distance yourself from any means of suicide. If you are thinking of taking an overdose, give your medicines to someone who can give them to you one day at a time. Remove any dangerous objects or weapons from your home.

3. Avoid using alcohol or other drugs.

4. Avoid doing things you're likely to fail at or find difficult until you're feeling better. Know what your present limits are and don't try to go beyond them until you feel better. Set realistic goals for yourself and work at them slowly, one step at a time.

5. Make a written schedule for yourself every day and stick to it no matter what. Set priorities for the things that need to be done first. Cross things out on your schedule as you finish them. A written schedule gives you a sense of predictability and control. Crossing out tasks as you complete them gives a feeling of accomplishment.

6. In your daily schedule don't forget to schedule at least two 30-minute periods for activities which, in the past, have given you some pleasure such as: listening to music, playing a musical instrument, meditating, relaxation exercises, needlework, reading a book or magazine, taking a warm bath, sewing, writing, shopping, playing games, watching your favorite DVD or video, gardening, playing with your pet, participating in a hobby, taking a drive or a walk.

7. Take care of your physical health. Eat a well-balanced diet. Don't skip meals. Get as much sleep as you need, and go out for one or two 30-minute walks each day.

8. Make sure you spend at least 30-minutes a day in the sun. Bright light is good for everyone with depression.

9. You may not feel very social but make yourself talk to other people. Whether you talk about your feelings or about any other topic, reducing your social isolation is likely to be helpful.

Remember that while it may feel as if it will never end, depression is not a permanent condition.

Closing

Close with a statement that describes short term next steps (i.e., "I'll need to contact your parents to talk about . . ." or, "You will be suspended for two days, then we'll . . ."). Try to determine client's affect or mood prior to his/her departure, and alert others if necessary.

Moderate Risk

If the client has had suicidal thoughts but does not seem likely to hurt himself in the near future, the risk is more moderate. If abuse or neglect is involved, staff should proceed as in the high-risk process. If there is no evidence of abuse, the parents should still be called to come in. They should be encouraged to take their child for an immediate evaluation.

Follow-Up

It is important to document all actions taken. If you have access to other professionals meet with them after the incident to go over the situation.

When faced with a child or adolescent threatening suicide, always take the threat seriously, go over the list of risk factors to determine if the threat may be imminent, and take the actions already prescribed. If you believe that there is no immediate threat of danger or if you are offering care after a suicide attempt, two main strategies to use are working with coping statements and problem-solving.

Helpful Coping Statements

Directions:

Tell the troubled youth that it is important to have some helpful coping statements which you can read to yourself, or remind yourself of in times of stress. Some examples might be:

- Today is a bad day, but it will pass. If I use the skills I have learned, it need only be a temporary step backwards.
- I have been here before, but this time I know what I have to do to stop it from getting worse.
- Everyone has bad days; mine can be a little worse. I just need to keep on track with my skills and tomorrow will be better.
- Things feel much worse today. This means I need to go back to my intervention techniques and start again. This will help me feel better.

Step 1: Explain to the young person that s/he will find it helpful to write his or her own helpful coping statements and that s/he may wish to write them on a sheet and keep them (e.g., in their wallet or purse) so that when s/he is feeling like they've taken a step backwards, they can pull out the sheet and read their helpful coping statements.

My helpful coping statements

1. _____
2. _____
3. _____
4. _____
5. _____
6. _____
7. _____
8. _____
9. _____
10. _____

Step 2: *What do I do if I start to find the going gets tougher?*

Explain to the client that when people feel depressed, they often start withdrawing from other people and stop doing things, isolating themselves to a degree. Unfortunately, although this is understandable, it only acts to compound their feelings of depression by cutting them off from any achievements or positive contact with others.

Tell them that there will be times when they may have more to deal with and may find the going harder. However, at such times, it is even more important to keep doing as many of the things that they would normally do, as possible. This is when it is most important to try to schedule activities that they need to do, as well as to schedule pleasant activities for themselves. Tell them to make sure that they don't go back to bed and close themselves off from the world and others. Let them know that it is important to keep doing things, even if they do less than they normally would. Doing something is better than doing nothing.

Step 3: *My thinking is not helping me.*

Explain that if they are beginning to feel like they are slipping backwards, that they need to take some time to examine their thinking. When people start to feel more depressed, they start to think more negatively, and they expect the worse. Explain that they often hold unrealistic expectations for themselves and others that are difficult to meet, leaving them feeling dissatisfied or guilty.

Have the client start monitoring his or her mood. The directions to give would be " Keep a diary of how you feel each day, and when you feel down, record what is going on around you (i.e. the situation). Include the thoughts you have about that situation or whatever else is going through your mind that is linked to your depressed feelings."

Step 4: *What supports do I need to put in place to keep from slipping backwards?*

Is there a particular friend who you can call? Is it time to schedule another appointment with your doctor or mental health professional?

This is what I will do:

_____

_____

_____

_____

_____

_____

_____

_____

_____

The Steps of Problem Solving

Directions:

Explain to the child: In order to solve a problem, you must ask and answer the following questions:

1. What is the problem?

2. What are some solutions? For each solution ask:

    a. Is it safe?

    b. How might people feel?

    c. Is it fair?

    d. Will it work?

3. Chose a solution and use it.

4. Is it working? If not, what can I do now?

Identifying the Problem

The first step in problem solving is identifying the problem. In order to do that, you must learn to look for and identify clues. Clues involve determining how you are acting and feeling and how others are acting and feeling.

- How does our body show that we are mad?

- How does our body show that we are sorry?

- How does our body show that we are happy?

- How does our body show that we are surprised?

- How does our body show that we are afraid?

- How does our body show that we are disgusted?

- How does our body show that we are guilty?

- How does our body show that we are interested?

Let's Learn to Detect Clues

The counselor will tell the youth that they are going to play a game. The counselor will say, " I am going to act out some different problems. I want you to think out loud to figure out what the problem might he. You can think out loud by saying what is going on and what clues you see.

Counselor models: thinking out loud while a s/he pantomimes looking for a lost dollar bill by acting out looking for the dollar and saying (for example), "He Is frowning and pacing back and forth. He seems upset and worried. He is looking in his pockets for something. He is looking on the ground. Maybe he lost something. Since he looked in his pocket, maybe he lost some money. I know, I'll ask him to find out." (To student) "What is the problem?"

Then have the client act out:

1. Waiting for someone who is late.

2. Trying to write with a pen that doesn't work.

While the child is acting this out, the counselor will give the clues out loud about the determining the problem.

Choosing a Solution

The counselor will tell the child, "In the last lesson you learned to ask and answer, 'What is the problem?' This is called *thinking out loud*. Let's look at a situation. Dory is a new girl who just moved into a neighborhood. She would like to play with a group of friends who are outside but she does not know what to do."

1. What is the problem? (Dory wants to play with the kids, but she has just moved into the neighborhood and doesn't know them very well. The kids haven't noticed her.) Today we will think out loud by *asking and answering* "What are some solutions?"

Solutions are ideas for solving a problem.

2. Let's think of all the things Dory could do. (Ask to play; hope that they notice her; find out what they're doing; push her way into the group.) (Note: Continue to probe by saying "That's one idea. What else could she do?" If they don't suggest "talking to them" or something similar, suggest it yourself.)

We have lots of ideas about what Dory could do. I am going to pretend I am Dory and think out loud to answer the question "What are some solutions?" Between each solution I want you to say OR. "What are some solutions? I could _____ OR I could _____ OR I could . . ."

Coming up with as many solutions as you can think of is called *brainstorming*.

Now we have several solutions Dory could use. There are four questions we can ask ourselves when we are deciding which solution to use: *Is it safe? How might people feel? Is it fair? Will it work?*

Let's ask these questions about each solution. I am going to model Dory thinking out loud for one solution:

"Let's see, what might happen if I push my way into the group?"

- Is it safe? Pushing might not be safe—someone could get hurt.
- How might people feel? Pushing might cause the kids to feel mad at me and I might feel embarrassed.
- Is it fair? Pushing is not fair.
- Will it work? It probably won't work because the kids wouldn't like me pushing them.

Now I would like you to pretend you are Dory and think out loud for each of the other solutions we came up with.

Now we need to choose a solution. Choosing a solution is the fourth step in solving a problem.

Now that we have thought about each solution, which solution would you choose? Why?

Now, at times you have made statements like "I wish I were dead." This happens sometimes when there is a problem that seems overwhelming. When you face such a problem, will you try to see if you can solve the problem instead of thinking that it would be better to die? Will you promise this?

My promise is: _____

_____

Signed: _____ Date: _____

(Client signature)

Giving Bad Thoughts Away

Directions:

When a child has thoughts that contain suicidal ideation, you need to teach the child to give the thoughts away. You will need a little box that the child should decorate and can keep and a set of blank cards (approximately twelve, small enough to fit into the box) or slips of paper.

Talk to the child about how we all have worries and that putting them away can help to get rid of them so that we can get on with life. Ask the child to decorate the box in any manner and talk about where the box of worries can live. The box needs to be some distance away from the child to illustrate the point that she does not have to carry her worries with her. For example, they could be deep in a cupboard or in another room. If the child is worrying about matters that adults should be concerned about (for example, if parents keep fighting and this upsets the child), it is appropriate to give the box each day to the caregiver when it is completed. This will illustrate to the child that the adults should be carrying that responsibility. Of course, the counselor should talk to the caregivers to ensure that they are responsible enough to understand their role in the exercise and in the child's life.

Next, take the set of cards and ask the child about the worry she would like to put away. Write each worry down on a separate card or piece of paper. Then, ritually, have the child put the worry in the box, giving positive reasons why she need not be concerned about them. Now put the lid down. The child may like to seal the box with some tape or a ribbon. Finally, put the box away together in the place already discussed, or give it to the caregiver if the place is at home. The adult caregiver then has the responsibility ensuring the box is put in the place the child has chosen.

Some children like to leave the box with the therapist. This can be useful if you plan to work on the worries with the child in the next session.

With all children and adolescents suicide threats should be taken seriously and evaluation should be carried out by a qualified assessor. That does not mean that counselors and other mental health professional should stay away from such children. If medicines are prescribed or a psychiatrist takes over care of the young person, a counselor can ask to work in conjunction with that professional to see if there are services that he or she can provide. It does take a village to raise a child in today's society.

Conclusion

This book examines incidence rates, diagnostic and statistical categories, best practice guidelines and practical treatment interventions for depressive disorders relating to children and adolescents. This book may serve as a guide and provide treatment possibilities to those in the mental health field. The treatments are not exhaustive but do stretch to stay within the best treatment guidelines for depressive disorder and bring the therapy down to the level of children and adolescents.

These interventions can be used to alleviate the symptoms of other mood disorders. Just match the technique or intervention to the symptoms of the disorder. I would encourage all of you to also check your bag of tools for other interventions that fit the best practice guidelines and that work with children and adolescents. In no time at all, with consistent use in sessions with young clients, you'll have them saying,

"I feel better now!"

References

Abramson, L. Y, Metalsky, G. I., & Alloy, L. B. (1989). Hopelessness depression: A theory-based subtype of depression. *Psychological Review, 96,* 358–372.

Abramson, L. Y, Seligman, M. E. P., & Teasdale, L. (1978). Learned helplessness in humans: Critique and reformulation. *Journal of Abnormal Psychology, 87,* 49–74.

American Academy Child and Adolescent Psychiatry, (1998). Practice parameters for the assessment and treatment of children and adolescents with depressive disorders. *Journal American Academy Child and Adolescent Psychiatry, 37.*

American Psychiatric Association, (2000). Diagnostic and statistical manual of mental disorders, 4th edition (*DSM-IV*). Washington, DC: American Psychiatric Association

Auger, R. (2005, Apr). School-based interventions for students with depressive disorders. *Professional School Counseling, 8 (4),* 344.

Beardslee, W.R., Wright, E.J., Salt, P., Drezner, K., Gladstone, T.R., Versage, E.M., & Rothberg, P.C., (1997). Examination of children's responses to two preventive intervention strategies over time. *Journal of the American Academy of Child and Adolescent Psychiatry, 36,*196–204

Beck, A. T. (1976). *Cognitive therapy and the emotional disorders.* New York: International Universities Press.

Beck, A. T., Rush, A. J., Shaw, B. F., & Emery, G. (1979). *Cognitive therapy of depression.* New York: Guilford Press.

Beck, J. S. (1995). *Cognitive therapy: Basics and beyond.* New York: Guilford Press.

Bernard, M.E., & Joyce, M.R. (1984). *Rational-Emotive Therapy with children and adolescents: Theory, treatment strategies, preventative methods.* New York: Wiley.

Birmaher, B., Ryan, N.D., Williamson, D., Brent, D., Kaufman, J., Dahl, R., Perel, J., & Nelson, B., (1996). Childhood and adolescent depression: A review of the past 10 years–Part I. *Journal of the American Academy Child and Adolescent Psychiatry*, 35,1427–1439

Birmaher, B., Ryan, N.D., Williamson, D.E., Brent, D.A., & Kaufman, J., (1996). Childhood and adolescent depression: A review of the past 10 years—Part II. *Journal of the American Academy Child and Adolescent Psychiatry*, 35, 1575–1583

Birmaher, B., Waterman, G.S., Ryan, N.D., Perel, J., McNabb, J., Balach, L., Beaudry, M.B., Nasr, F.N., Karambelkar, J., Elterich, G., Quintana, B., Williamson, D.E., & Rao, U., (1998). A randomized controlled trial of amitriptyline vs. placebo for adolescents with "treatment-resistant" major depression. *Journal of the American Academy Child and Adolescent Psychiatry*, 37, 527–535

Bisignano, J. & McElmurry, M. (1987). *The changing years: My journal of personal Growth.* Carthage, IL: Good Apple, Inc.

Boulos, C., Kutcher, S., Gardner, D., & Young, E., (1992). An open naturalistic trial of fluoxetine in adolescents and young adults with treatment-resistant major depression. *Journal of Child and Adolescent Psychopharmacology*, 2, 103–111

Burns, D. D. (1999). *Feeling good: The new mood therapy.* New York: Morrow.

Brent, D.A., Perper, J.A., Moritz, G., Allman, C., Friend, A., Roth, C., Schweers, J., Balach, L., & Baugher, M., (1993). Psychiatric risk factors for adolescent suicide: A case-control study. *Journal of the American Academy of Child and Adolescent Psychiatry*, 32, 21–529

Brent, D.A., (1995). Risk factors for adolescent suicide and suicidal behavior: Mental and substance abuse disorders, family environmental factors, and life stress. *Suicide Life and Threatening Behavior*, 25, 52–63

Brent, D.A., Holder, D., Kolko, D., Birmaher, B., Baugher, M., Roth, C., Iyengar, S., & Johnson, B. (1997). A clinical psychotherapy trial for adolescent depression comparing cognitive, family, and supportive treatments. *Archives of General Psychiatry*, 54, 877–885

British National Formulary, (2000, March). No. 39. London: The Pharmaceutical Press, 191–3

Bums, D. D. (1999). *Feeling good : The new mood therapy.* New York: Morrow.

Cantor, C., (2001). Surgeon General targets children's mental health: A national action agenda. [Online] Available: http://health.medscape.com/ex/viewarticle/230617.

Capuzzi, J., & Ross, N., (1999). *Youth at risk: A prevention resource for counselors, teachers, and parents.* New York: Brooks/Cole.

Center for Mental Health Services/ORC MACRO. (2004). *National evaluation of the comprehensive community mental health service for children and their families program.* 1990–2000 Grant Communities Data Profile Reports. Atlanta, GA.

Chambers, W.J., Puig-Antich, J., Tabrizi, M.A., & Davies, M. (1982). Psychotic symptoms in prepubertal major depressive disorder. *Archives of General Psychiatry,* 39, 921–927

Christian Woman Today. (2004). *The language of color.* Retrieved September 22, 2004 from, http://www.christianwomentoday.com/home/color.html

Clarke, G.N., Hawkins, W., Murphy, M., Sheeber, L.B., Lewinsohn, P.M., & Seeley, J.R. (1995). Targeted prevention of unipolar depressive disorder in an at-risk sample of high school adolescents: A randomized trial of a group cognitive intervention. *Journal of the American Academy of Child and Adolescent Psychiatry,* 34, 312–321

Corey, G. (2001). *Theory and practice of counseling and psychotherapy* (6th ed.). Belmont, CA: Wadsworth.

Depression Guideline Panel, (1993). *Depression in Primary Care*: Vol I. *Treatment of Major Depression. Clinical Practice Guideline.* Rockville, MD: U.S. Department of Health and Human Services, Public Health Service, Agency for Health Care Policy and Research

Ellis, A. (1962). *Reason and emotion in psychotherapy.* New York: Lyle Stuart.

Ellis, A. (1971a). *Growth through reason.* North Hollywood, CA: Wilshire.

Ellis, A. (1971b). *Humanistic psychotherapy.* New York: Crown.

Ellis, A. (1980). An overview of the clinical theory of Rational-Emotive Therapy. In R. Grieger & J. Byrd (Eds.), *Rational-Emotive Therapy: A skills-based approach.* New York: Van Nostrand.

Elkind, D. (1967). Egocentrism in adolescence. *Child development, 38,* 1025–1034.

Elkind, D. (1970). *Children and adolescents: Interpretative essays on Jean Piaget.* New York: Oxford Press

Emslie, G.J., Rush, A.J., Weinberg, W.A., Kowatch, R.A., Hughes, C.W., Carmody, T., & Rintelmann, J. (1997). A double-blind randomized, placebo-controlled trial of fluoxetine in children and adolescents with depression. *Archives of General Psychiatry,* 54, 1031–1037

Emslie, G.J., & Mayes, T.L.,(1999, Mar 11). Depression in children and adolescents: A guide to diagnosis and treatment. CNS Drugs, 3, 181–189

Fergusson, D.M., Lynsky, M.T., Horwood, L.J., (1996). Childhood sexual abuse and psychiatric disorder in young adulthood: I. Prevalence of sexual abuse and factors associated with sexual abuse. *Journal of American Academy of Child and Adolescent Psychiatry,* 35, 1355–1364

Findling, R.L. ,(1996). Open-label treatment of comorbid depression and attentional disorders with co-administration of serotonin reuptake inhibitors and psychostimulants in children, adolescents, and adults: A case series. *Journal of Child and Adolescent Psychomarmacology,* 6, 165–175

Findling, R.L., Reed, M..D., & Blumer, J.L. (1999 Jul–Sep). Pharmacological treatment of depression in children and adolescents. Paediatric Drugs,1(3), 161–182.

Fleming, J.E., & Offord, D.R., (1990). Epidemiology of childhood depressive disorders: A critical review. *Journal of the American Academy of Child and Adolescent Psychiatry,* 29, 571–580

Frank, E., Prien, R.F., Jarret, R.B., Keller, M.B., Kupfer, D.J., Lavori, P.W., Rush, A.J., & Weissman, M.M. (1991). Conceptualization and rationale for consensus definitions of terms in Major depressive disorder. Remission, recovery, relapse and recurrence. *Archives of General Psychiatry,*48, 851–855

Fristad, M.A,, Gavazzi, S.M., Centolella, D.M., & Soldano, K.W. (1996). Psychoeducation: A promising intervention strategy for families of children and adolescents with mood disorders. *Contemporary Family Therapy,* 18, 371–383

Geller, B., Cooper, T., Graham, D., Marsteller, F.A., & Bryant, D.M. (1990). Double-blind placebo-controlled study of nortriptyline in depressed adolescents using a "fixed plasma level" design. *Psychopharmacology Bulletin,* 26, 85–90

Geller, B. (1994). Should tricyclic antidepressants be prescribed to depressed children and adolescents? *Current Opinion Psychiatry,* 7, 301–303

Goldman, W. (1999). Depression. *Keep kids healthy.* Retrieved May 16, 2005, from http://www.keepkidshealthy.com.

Gould, M.S., Fishe,r P., Parides, M., Flory, M., & Shaffer, D. (1996). Psychosocial risk factors of child and adolescent completed suicide. *Archives of General Psychiatry*, 53, 1155–1162.

Hendin, H., Lipschitz, A., Maltsberger, J.T., Haas, A.P., & Wynecoop, S. (2000) Therapists' reactions to patients' suicides. *American Journal of Psychiatry.*158:2022–2027.

Hobday, A., & Ollier, K. (1999). *Creative therapy with children and adolescents.* Atascadero, CA: Impact Publishers, Inc.

Holistic Psychology (n.d.). *Progressive muscle relaxation for children.* Retrieved September 8, 2004, from http://www.yourfamilyclinic.com/adhd/relax.htm

Jaycox, L.H., Reivich, K.J., Gillham, J., & Seligman, M.E. (1994). The prevention of depressive symptoms in school children. *Behavior Research Therapy*, 32, 801–816

Jacobs, D.G., Brewer, M,. & Klein-Benheim, M. (1998). Suicide assessment: an overview and recommended protocol. In: Jacobs, D., ed. *Harvard Medical School Guide to Assessment and Intervention in Suicide.* San Francisco, CA: Jossey-Bass; 1998:3–39.

Kadson, H. G., & Schaefer, C. E. (2000). *Short-Term play therapy for children.* New York: The Guilford Press.

Kahn, J.S., Kehle, T.J., Jenson, W.R., & Clark, E., (1990). Comparison of cognitive-behavioral, relaxation, and self-modeling interventions for depression among middle-school students. *School Psychology Review*, 19, 196–211

Kashani, J.H., Beck, N.C., Hoeper, E.W., Fallahi, C., Corcoran, C.M., McAllister. J.A., Rosenberg, T.K., & Reid, J.C., (1987a). Psychiatric disorders in a community sample of adolescents. *American Journal of Psychiatry*, 144, 584–589

Kashani, J.H., Carlson, G.A., Beck, N.C., Hoeper, E.W., Corcoran, C.M., McAllister, J.A., Fallahi, C., Rosenberg, T.K., & Reid, J.C. (1987b), Depression, depressive symptoms, and depressed mood among a community sample of adolescents. *American Journal of Psychiatry*, 144, 931–934

Kessler, r., Nelson, C., McGonagle, K., Edlund, J., Frank, R., & Leaf, R. (1996). The epidemiology of co-occurring addictive and mental disorders: Implications for prevention and service utilization. *American Journal of Orthopsychiatry*, 66, 17–31.

Kovacs, M., (1992). *Children's depression inventory (CDI) manual.* North Tonawanda, NY: Multi-Health Systems, Inc.

Kovacs, M., & Gatsonis, C. (1994). Secular trends in age at onset of major depressive disorder in a clinical sample of children. *Journal of Psychiatric Research*, 28, 319–329.

Kovacs, M., Obrosky, S., Gatsonis, C., & Richards, C. (1997). First-episode of major depressive and dysthymic disorder in childhood: Clinical and sociodemographic factors in recovery. *Journal of American Academy of Child and Adolescent Psychiatry*, 36, 777–784

Kroll, L., Harrington, R., Jayson, D., Fraser, J., & Gowers, S. (1996). Pilot study of continuation cognitive-behavioral therapy for major depression in adolescent psychiatric patients. *Journal of American Academy of Child and Adolescent Psychiatry*, 35, 1156–1161

Lewinsohn, P.M., Clarke, G.N., Hops, H., & Andrews, J. (1990). Cognitive-behavioral group treatment for depressed adolescents. *Behavior Therapy*, 21, 385–401

Lewinsohn, P.M., Hops, H., Roberts, R.E., Seeley, J.R., & Andrews, J.A., (1993a). Adolescent psychopathology: I. Prevalence and incidence of depression and other *DSM-III-R* disorders in high school students. *Journal of Abnormal Psychology*, 102, 133–144

Lewinsohn, P.M., Rohde, P., & Seeley, J.R., (1993b). Psychosocial characteristics of adolescents with a history of suicide attempt. *Journal of the American Academy of Child and Adolescent Psychiatry*, 32, 60–68

Lewinsohn, P.M., Clarke, G.N., Seeley, J.R., & Rohde, P. (1994). Major depression in community adolescents: Age at onset, episode duration, and time to recurrence. *Journal of the American Academy of Child and Adolescent Psychiatry*, 33, 809–818

Manaster, G.J. (1977). *Adolescent development and the life tasks.* Boston: Allyn & Bacon

Mandoki, M.W., Tapia, M.R., Tapia, M. A., Sumner, G.S., & Parker, J.L. (1997). Venlafaxine in the treatment of children and adolescents with major depression. *Psychopharmacology Bulletin*, 33, 149–154

Marton, P., Churchard, M., Kutcher, S., & Koremblum, M. (1991). Diagnostic utility of the Beck Depression Inventory with adolescent psychiatric outpatients and inpatients. *Canadian Journal of Psychiatry*, 36, 428–431

Marton, P., & Kutcher, S. (1995). The prevalence of cognitive distortion in depressed adolescents. *Journal of Psychiatry and Neuroscience*, 20, 33–38

Mind Tools. (2004). *Decision tree analysis.* Retrieved October 3, 2004, from http://www.mindtools.com/pages/article/newTED_04.htm

Mitchell, J., McCauley, E., Burle, P.M., & Mass, S.J. (1988). Phenomenology of depression in children and adolescents. *Journal of American Academy of Child Adolescent Psychiatry*, 1, 12–20

New Freedom Commission on Mental Health. (2003). *Achieving the Promise: Transforming Mental Health Care in America, Final Report.* Department of Human Services Publication Number SMA-0303832.

NGA Center for Best Practices. (2005). *Youth Suicide Prevention: Strengthening State Policies and School-Based Strategies.*

Padesky, C. A. (1994). Schema change processes in cognitive therapy. *Clinical Psychology and Psychotherapy, 1,* 267–278.

Reynolds, W.M., & Coates, K.I. (1986). A comparison of cognitive-behavioral therapy and relaxation training for the treatment of depression in adolescents. *Journal of Consulting and Clinical Psychology,* 54, 653–660

Reinecke, M.A., Ryan, N.E., & DuBois, D.L. (1998). Cognitive-behavioral therapy of depression and depressive symptoms during adolescence: A review and meta-analysis. *Journal of American Academy of Child and Adolescent Psychiatry,* 37, 26–34

Riethmayer, J. (1993). *About life & loss.* Bryan, TX: BJR Enterprises.

Roberts, R.E., Lewinsohn, P.M., Seeley, J.R. (1991). Screening for Adolescent Depression: A comparison of depression scales. *Journal of the American Academy of Child and Adolescent Psychiatry,* 30, 8–66

Ryan, N.D., Puig-Antich, J., Ambrosini, P., Rabinovich, H., Robinson, D., Nelson, B., Iyengar, S., & Twomey, J. (1987). The clinical picture of major depression in children and adolescents. *Archives of General Psychiatry,* 44, 854–861

Ryan, N., Puig-Antich, J., Rabinovich, H., Fied, J., Ambrosini, P., Meyer, V., Torres, D., Dachille, S., & Mazzie, D. (1988a). MAOIs in adolescent major depression unresponsive to tricyclic antidepressant. *Journal of the American Academy of Child and Adolescent Psychiatry,* 27, 755–758

Ryan, N., Meyer, V., Dachille, S., Mazzie, D., & Puig-Antich, J., (1988b). Lithium antidepressant augmentation in TCA-refractory depression in adolescents. *Journal of the American Academy of Child and Adolescent Psychiatry,* 27, 371–376

Ryan, N.D., Williamson, D.E., Iyengar, S., Orvaschel, H., Reich, T., Dahl, R.E., & Puig-Antich, J. (1992). A secular increase in child and adolescent onset affective disorder. *Journal of the American Academy of Child and Adolescent Psychiatry,*31, 600–605

Salle, F.R., Vrindavanam, N.S., Deas-Nesmith, D., Carson, S.W., & Sethuraman, G. (1997). Pulse intravenous clomipramine for depressed adolescents: A double-blind controlled trial. *American Journal of Psychiatry, 154,* 668–673

Teplin, L. (2002). Psychiatric disorders in youth in juvenile detention. *Archives of General Psychiatry, 59.* 1133–1143.

Thase, M.E., & Rush, A.J. (1995). Treatment-resistant depression. In: *Psychopharmacology: The Fourth Generation of Progress,* F.E. Bloom , & D.J. Kupfer , Eds. New York: Raven Press, pp 1081–1097

Thase, M.E., Fava, M., Halbreich, U., Kocsis, J.H., Koran, L., Davidson, J., Rosenbaum, J., & Harrison, W. (1996). A placebo-controlled, randomized clinical trial comparing sertraline and imipramine for the treatment of dysthymia. *Archives of General Psychiatry, 53,* 77–784

Thase, M.E., & Kupfer, D.J. (1996). Recent developments in the pharmacotherapy of mood disorders. *Journal of Consulting and Clinical Psychology, 64,* 646–659

U.S. Department of Health and Human Services. (1999) *Mental Health: A Report of the Surgeon General.* U.S. Department of Health and Human Services, Substance Abuse and Mental Health Services Administration, Center for Mental Health Services, National Institutes of Health, National Institute of Mental Health. Rockville, MD.

U.S. Department of Health and Human Services, (2003). *AFCARS Report: Preliminary FY 2001 Estimates as of March 2003.* Washington, DC.

Vostanis, P., Feehan, C., Grattan, E., & Bickerton, W. (1996). A randomized controlled outpatient trial of cognitive-behavioral treatment for children and adolescents with depression: Nine-month follow-up. *Journal of Affective Disorders, 40,* 105–116

Western Washington University. (2003). *Five finger exercise.* Retrieved October 14, 2004, from http://www.wwu.edu/chw/counseling/specific_topics/ stress_bio/five.html

Wilens, T.E., Spencer, T.J., Biederman, J., & Schleifer, D. (1997). Case study: Nefazodone for juvenile mood disorders. *Journal of the American Academy of Child and Adolescent Psychiatry, 36,* 481–485

Young, J. E. (1990). *Schema-focused cognitive therapy for personality disorders: A schema-focused approach.* Sarasota, FL: Professional Resource Exchange.